JIGSAW
PIECES

And the Main Thing is...
Learning

Keeping the focus on learning – for pupils *and* teachers

By Mike Hughes

Foreword by Paul Ginnis

Education
Training and
Support

Published by Education Training and Support

P O Box 797

Cheltenham

GL52 6WR

ISBN 978-0-9546290-3-8

Every effort has been made to contact copyright holders of materials reproduced in this book. The publisher apologises for any omissions and will be pleased to rectify them at the earliest opportunity.

Editor: **Gina Walker**

Design and layout: **Colin Barker**

Printed in the UK by: **Gomer Press, Llandysul, Ceredigion, Wales**

Contents

Acknowledgements — 4

Foreword by Paul Ginnis — 5

Setting the scene — 9

Section 1: Teacher as learner — 19

Section 2: Defining learning — 65

Section 3: A lesson template based explicitly on learning — 81

Section 4: Unpacking learning — 107

Section 5: Case studies – Beyond good — 201

The end of the beginning — 239

Further reading — 251

Jigsaw Pieces — 254

ETS services — 255

Acknowledgements

Many people have contributed to this book, either directly or indirectly, and I am grateful to all those who have been involved in any way, shape or form. Many, many thanks are due to:

- all those schools listed below who have agreed to share their story and to the following people who made the time to put pen to paper: Karl Sampson, Ricky Perrott, Mark Kenny, Pete Weir, Denise Walker, Becky Pearce, Rob Edwards, Fiona Manser, Andy Love, Tom Dore, Sue Dodd, Sarah Bainton, Therese Allen, Robin Precey, Jan Molyneux, Penny Stevens, Douglas Greig, Kate Battersby, Sue Kershaw, Graham Tyrer and Colin Bradley.

- all those schools and teachers who have been using the tools and approaches outlined in this book. Their feedback has been invaluable.

- Paul Ginnis for agreeing to write the foreword. Reading Paul's *A Guide to Student-Centred Learning* in the mid-eighties was a significant moment in my early career. The book helped give form to many of the nebulous thoughts swirling around my head at the time and provided the vocabulary and structure that I was beginning to search for. Little did I know then that the author would one day write the foreword to a book that I had written! At the risk of being gushy, it is a real thrill – it feels a bit like having Alan Ball or Phil Bennett come to watch me play.

- Gina Walker and Colin Barker for their expertise and patience; if they were frustrated by the last minute alterations, they were kind enough not to show it.

- Rach, Ben and Sam – for their tolerance, patience and encouragement. Only they know the real story and I'm not sure who is looking forward to the book being finished most, them or me. For as was the case with our own children, the conception of this book was very much easier than the actual birth; not only was it infinitely more enjoyable it was also, if truth be told, significantly quicker.

I would also like to acknowledge the role that Johann Sebastian Bach, Jaffa Cakes and Andy Johnson played in keeping my spirits high while the writing was in full swing.

Schools that have contributed to this book:
- Arbourthorne Primary School, Sheffield
- Ash Green School, Warwickshire
- Y Bont Faen Primary School, Cowbridge
- Canterbury Christ Church University
- Castle Vale School and Performing Arts College, Birmingham
- The Cavendish School and Sports College, Hemel Hempstead
- City Academy Bristol
- Ecclesall Junior School, Sheffield
- Farlingaye High School, Suffolk
- Gorse Hill Infant School, Swindon
- Methwold High School, Norfolk
- Old Cleeve C of E First School, Washford
- saltash.net community school, Saltash
- Somervale School, Midsomer Norton
- St John Lloyd Catholic Comprehensive School, Llanelli
- Tring School
- Waingels College, Reading
- Warwickshire Inclusion Network
- Wychall Primary School, Birmingham

Foreword

By Paul Ginnis

This book is of great importance to the nation. It provides a compass direction, a route map and a set of tactics that will enable us to achieve the educational goals that matter most.

It is reassuring to know that Mike Hughes has an authoritative overview. Over the years, from a wide variety of standpoints, he has observed the shifts in educational policy and practice and has mapped them against the bigger picture of our increasing understanding of the learning process. Many times he has explained to us the important and self-evident truth of constructivism: that learning only truly occurs when learners make sense of the learning for themselves.

Ever the realist, Mike has skilfully translated this modern understanding of learning into the language of our times. The political drives to raise attainment, narrowly measured, and the attendant pressures of accountability expressed through league tables and inspection, have forced managers to focus on the quality of teaching in their schools. Teaching has been tidied up and, in the worst cases, moulded into predictable shapes, codified, mechanised and unified. The 'national strategies' have aided this process by exerting a moral and peer pressure to adopt 'samey' methods. In some cases, these have constrained teaching, particularly where schools have imposed rather crude structures such as 'the three-part lesson'. Certain teaching formulae have become widespread and, at worst, have resulted in rituals that have tended to suck the lifeblood out of best practice. True, these prescriptions might have made weaker teachers better, but at a price. In an attempt to raise the floor, it could be argued that the ceiling has been lowered.

Mike Hughes' writing has cleverly worked with this orthodoxy and subtly expanded our understanding and implementation of its key themes. For example, lesson observation: Mike has provided tools that shift the focus from teaching to learning. Another example, lesson structure: accepting that clear thinking and planning are important, Mike has provided a four-part experience as opposed to a three-part cycle that is grounded in learning theory. This new book is in the same vein; it locates a refined and distilled understanding of learning (we've moved on from the froth and bubble of VAK) within the current culture of our profession. It is a realistic piece of work that nudges our thinking forward. *And the Main Thing is ... Learning* does not lambast; it does not criticise or destroy. Rather, it questions, challenges and connects. The book looks back and looks forward; it consolidates the territory we have gained and provides further bridges for us to cross as we continue the journey from where we have been to where we need to go.

This book gives us a clear idea of the way forward. The key is to be found on page 112, the TIMS Grid. Here is the shift from past to future tense. Mike challenges us to think about the kind of teaching (box D) that will enable students to make sense of, and manage, learning for themselves. The logic is obvious: as soon as we accept a sound approach to learning, one based on constructivism, the psychology of motivation and the central place of emotion, there have to be concomitant changes to the way business is conducted in the classroom – the teaching paradigm must alter.

This is where things get scary, for two reasons. First, 'the ghost of teaching past' begins to appear; terms like 'facilitation' and 'student-centred learning' send shivers down the spines of some. Second, teachers don't necessarily know how to operate the new model; the fine skills of co-constructed learning have been trained out of them under the *ancien régime* (and in the case of younger teachers, were never trained into them in the first place). There is understandable resistance at several levels. Apart from the skill deficit, many teachers feel that they don't have permission to branch out in a new direction; something that QCA under the curriculum leadership of Mick Waters is working hard to reverse.

Mike defines the kind of teaching that proper learning requires. However, this style will only flourish if permission-from-the-top, resources, training (centred on skilled coaching and reflective practice) and conducive structures are provided. This means that there are several high-level, country-wide challenges to face if we are to stride forward in the direction that he proposes.

First, there is the challenge to clarify national educational priorities. Surely it is time to recognise that we are beholden, morally, to achieve more than good test and exam results. The momentum of 'learning to learn' initiatives across the country is an indication of the shift in perspective. There is a raft of social and economic reasons for pursuing broader educational outcomes and sooner or later a new political agenda will have to be set. At the moment, the healthy new shoots at grass-roots level are having to grow under a dark sky.

Second, there is the challenge to create locally relevant and integrated curricula. We are, I'm pleased to say, being encouraged by QCA to combine and customise the primary curriculum, to integrate literacy and numeracy and to reduce content and increase flexibility at KS3. Also, there are many positive and exciting experiments, especially in Y7, that integrate subjects and reconfigure timetables. The logic of high-profile movements such as personalised learning and schools for the future, along with the aspirations for community learning and integrated technology, if we dared to pursue it far enough, would take us to new and flexible structures.

Third, there is the challenge to re-assert creative, expansive and varied teaching methods, drawing on pedagogic models that have been pooh-poohed for the last two decades: experiential learning; discovery learning; investigative learning; student-centred learning; democratic learning and so on. Again, progress is being made. Play is coming back into fashion in the Early Years, as is the use of drama as a learning medium, and there is a national call for creativity.

Fourth, there is the challenge to create school leaders who are, first and foremost, leaders of learning. Progress in classroom methodology, turning good teachers into great, and in reinventing curriculum and school organisation, can only occur if the most powerful people in schools have a clear, learning-based vision and a conviction about the principles that underpin it.

The book you are holding in your hands encourages and informs these developments. It helps to resolve tensions – tensions between old and new ideas, tensions between varying priorities and paradigms, tensions between politics and professionalism. It does so by taking us forward gently, through logic and rational argument, and by presenting lots of workable ideas for classroom teachers and school managers that fit the current culture, but are based on principles fit for the future.

Paul Ginnis
October 2006

In many respects, we have reached the end of the beginning; for if phase one of the national drive to raise standards was to improve teaching, phase two is to *place learning at the heart of everything we do.*

Setting the scene

> *We are prisoners of our past. It is hard to think of things except in the way we have thought of them.*
>
> Albert Einstein

The context

Teaching standards have improved considerably in recent years and, if we use examination success as the yardstick, there has been a corresponding increase in attainment. Given the particular circumstances of the school and the nature of the catchment, the vast majority of teachers are doing a good job with the vast majority of children on the vast majority of occasions. The teaching profession as a whole is clearly performing at an impressively high level.

The challenge

> 1 To sustain the improvements of recent years.
> 2 To switch the focus from *teaching* to *learning*.

No matter how well teachers are doing, no one appears to be satisfied, and of the many challenges that face the profession as we move towards the second decade of the 21st century, none is more daunting than the imperative to sustain these improvements and to build from what is already a high base.

Although teachers and school leaders have faced the challenge to continually raise the bar and improve on existing levels of performance for a number of years now, the emphasis has changed. No longer are we seeking to eradicate poor and unsatisfactory performance in the classroom; that challenge has largely been met. We are now confronted by the arguably greater challenge of improving and developing high quality teaching still further. In short, **we are seeking to turn** *good* **into** *great*.

We are also seeking to switch the focus from teaching to learning. Government policy in recent years has been firmly based upon a concerted effort to improve *teaching*, with the assumption that improved teaching would lead to gains in examination success. As has already been suggested, this policy has largely been successful. Yet many would argue that better exam results were often achieved at the expense of *learning*. A plethora of initiatives, pressure for immediate measurable improvement and a suffocating climate of accountability have exerted a subtle, yet powerful influence on teachers to play safe, cover the curriculum and 'teach to the test', sacrificing learning and the longer-term investment of developing learning capacity for short-term examination and inspection success. Despite the rhetoric, the reality is that all too often examination results, 'pleasing the PANDA' and generally jumping through hoops have been our prime focus.

Will the strategies and policies that have enabled us to reach *good* and improve teaching be sufficient to help us move *beyond good* and promote learning?

It is important to acknowledge the significant number of notable exceptions to the generalisations made on the previous page. There are, of course, teachers and schools for whom learning and developing children as learners have always been the prime focus. It is also worth noting at this point that schools in which children both *learn* and *learn about learning* tend to do very well against national measures of success, for learning and examination success are not mutually exclusive.

Yet, up to now, the schools and teachers who have succeeded in keeping learning in the spotlight, confident that examination success would inevitably follow, have largely done so despite of, rather than because of, government policy. That is now changing and the national focus is firmly and explicitly upon learning. In many respects, we have reached the end of the beginning; for if phase one of the national drive to raise standards has been to focus upon improving teaching, phase two is to place learning at the heart of everything we do.

The question

The question that we need to address, therefore, is:

> Will the strategies and policies that have enabled us to get to *good* and improve teaching be sufficient to help us move *beyond* good and promote learning?

Is it to be more of the same, or do we need a change of emphasis if we are to break through the inevitable plateau of attainment and achievement?

Government strategy to improve teaching during the last decade has been characterised by:

- training
- monitoring
- pressure and accountability.

In order to build upon the undoubted success of recent years, do we simply need to provide more training, monitor performance and apply ever increasing pressure? Will the approaches that proved so effective in eradicating unsatisfactory teaching, developing a consistency in classroom practice and significantly raising attainment, continue to be effective as we seek to move from good to great? **Or do we need an altogether different approach?**

The argument

The central argument of this book is that a strategy based largely upon training, monitoring and applying pressure – which has taken us to *good* – will alone be insufficient to help schools and teachers move *beyond* good. For further improvement from such a high base demands an approach rooted in learning and, while training and monitoring may be effective and necessary management tools, they have precious little to do with learning. As its title suggests, this book argues that **learning must be the main thing**.

The main thing is to keep the main thing the main thing.

Stephen R Covey

And the main thing is ... *learning*

A large sign proclaiming, *And the main thing is ... learning* can be found at the entrance to saltash.net community school in Cornwall as a constant reminder that our core business as teachers is to *help children learn*. It is a mantra inspired by the quote from Stephen Covey opposite.

It is hardly a contentious claim! Indeed, there is arguably greater consensus than ever before that the core business of schools and teachers is learning. And yet, despite this almost unequivocal agreement that schools exist to promote learning, it is all too easy for the very thing that we are trying to foster to become side-tracked in the pressure-cooker, hundred-miles-an-hour world that is education.

The gist of Covey's argument is that successful institutions are those that succeed in keeping *the main thing the main thing* in the face of all the distractions, and that if we fail to make a *conscious* commitment to our goal we allow the sub-conscious influences to distract and inevitably divert us from the main thing.

This book is about how to keep learning as the main thing. It is based upon three discrete, yet inextricably linked, key principles:

> 1 **Everything in the organisation must be based *explicitly* upon learning.** Good schools are aligned, and display high degrees of internal consistency. This alignment must be based upon a shared understanding of, and commitment to, learning.
>
> 2 **Teachers must also be learners.** We cannot truly create a learning school or climate conducive to learning that excludes teachers. Learning must permeate the entire institution and not be confined to something we do with children.
>
> 3 **The deeper we understand learning and the learning process, the better able we are to facilitate it in others.**

> *Talk in classrooms is mainly about work, sometimes about performance, and rarely about learning. At best, 2% of classroom interactions are about learning and how it may be advanced ... try banning the word 'work' from your classroom and see what happens when you substitute the word 'learning' – effects can be electric!*

Chris Watkins et al, *NSIN Research Matters* 2002

The better we understand learning the better able we are to facilitate it in others.

About this book

This book will argue that in order to translate rhetoric into practice and meet the aspirations described on the previous pages, schools and teachers must take learning and:

- define it
- base lessons *explicitly* upon it
- reflect on it, analyse it, discuss it, unpack it – in order to deepen our understanding of it; because the better we understand learning and the learning process the better we are able to facilitate it in others.

The third bullet point above demands that teachers are learners too. However, it is all too easy to nod in agreement when it is suggested that teachers should also be learners and for phrases such as *teacher as reflective practitioner* to glibly trip off the tongue without fully digesting the implications of such statements. For if we are serious about teachers as learners, we need nothing less than a significant culture shift in which the emphasis on training and monitoring is replaced by a commitment to dialogue and professional reflection.

Such a culture will not just happen by chance; our goal must be to consciously create a culture of professional reflection in which teachers are encouraged to take risks, reflect, explore, swap and share. Two discrete, yet inextricably linked, dimensions lie at the heart of such a culture:

- coaching
- teacher as researcher.

Both are rooted in learning and involve individual teachers making personal meaning of their current reality, and in doing so deepening their understanding of learning and the learning process.

During the last decade or so, our collective interest in and understanding of learning has mushroomed, which in turn has led to fundamental changes in classroom practice. It was not too long ago that children were expected to learn in the way their teacher taught. Increasingly, teachers are now expected to teach in the way children – individual children – learn. Teaching is now seen as a response to learning and as our understanding of learning deepens and grows ever more sophisticated, pedagogy will continue to respond and evolve.

However, as much as we know about learning and facilitating it in others, there is still more that we don't know, and there remains an imperative to go on learning about learning … for the better we understand it, the better able we are to facilitate it in others.

Key principles

1 Everything in the organisation must be based *explicitly* upon learning.

2 Teachers must also be learners.

3 The deeper we understand learning and the learning process, the better able we are to facilitate it in others.

The book, in both style and content, attempts to reflect the principles outlined on the opposite page. It is written in five sections:

Section 1: Teacher as learner

Tweaking, Tweak of the Week at St John Lloyd Catholic Comprehensive School, The learning culture, Teacher as researcher, Non-judgemental data, Professional enquiry teams at Somervale School, Coaching, Case studies: Coaching at Methwold High School; Professional Development at Castle Vale Performing Arts College

Section 2: Defining learning

Key principles of learning, Generating a shared understanding of learning, A metaphor for learning, Teaching in the way children learn

Section 3: A lesson template based explicitly on learning

Basing lessons explicitly upon learning, The significance of reflection, A suggested learning structure, Observable indicators, Planning lessons or learning experiences? Adopting the 'four-phase' learning template at saltash.net community school, Using a learning template as a basis for professional development at City Academy Bristol, Impact of a learning template at Tring School, The Chinese dimension at Canterbury Christ Church University

Section 4: Unpacking learning – reflecting on the key middle part of the lesson

Learning more about learning, The TIMS grid, The difference between knowing and understanding, The role of the teacher, The role of the learner, The difference between receiving information and making sense of it, What does facilitating learning mean? When and how to intervene, The engagement triangle

Section 5: Case studies – Beyond good

Improving lessons from a high base, The 3 'E's – enthrall, entice, excite, The 3 'C's – curiosity, confusion, challenge, Exploring curiosity at Farlingaye High School, Developing cognitive conflict at saltash.net community school, Learner-led learning at Wychall Primary School

This book does not pretend to provide *the answer*. Indeed, one of its key messages is that learning involves making personal sense and therefore meaning cannot be given to another. **You have to learn about learning.**

In this spirit, material is offered as food for thought with the intention of stimulating professional reflection and debate, for it is only through professional reflection that we will succeed in placing learning at the heart of all we do and continue to move forward from an already high base.

Dyfal donc a dyr y garreg

Dyfal donc a dyr y garreg is an old Welsh proverb that, in English, means 'constant dripping wears the stone'. The reference to perseverance and the reminder that little things can make a big difference beautifully encapsulate the ***Tweak of the Week*** strategy employed by **St John Lloyd Comprehensive School** in Llanelli.

Tweak of the Week

The phrase was coined by Ricky Perrott, Assistant Head at the school with responsibility for learning, as a light-hearted way of keeping the idea of tweaking practice to the fore.

'Tweaking' practice is based upon the belief that most people are more likely to make and sustain small changes than large ones, and that significant change can occur through a series of small steps or 'tweaks'.

This simple philosophy had been the subject of an extended LEA three-day course that Ricky had attended back in 2003, which featured the four-phase lesson outlined in *Tweak to Transform* by Mike Hughes. On return to school, Ricky shared the basic ideas with the staff during an Inset day and wanted to find a way of reinforcing them without placing excessive additional demands on teachers.

Each week, a single tweak was identified and shared with all staff via the weekly bulletin. These tweaks were designed to consolidate individual elements within the four-phase model. A Teaching and Learning board was also set up in the staffroom – strategically placed above the photocopier – to amplify the bulletin tweaks.

Tweak of the Week has extended even further and now appears on the LEA's website, www.amdro.org.uk, and will soon be sent electronically to all staff at the school.

The strategy appears to be working. In 2004, HMI reported that:

- ***Teachers are confident and willing to improve, resulting in very positive attitudes being displayed by pupils towards their learning.***

- ***Lessons are well planned and employ varied activities which engage the pupils.***

Rumour has it that some teachers keep a *Tweak of the Week* scrapbook!

Section 1: Teacher as learner

> *Learning and teaching improve when teachers have the tools and grasp the value of being learners in their own classroom.*
>
> Professor John MacBeath

This section considers the following issues:
1 Tweaking
2 Done *to* / done *by*
3 The learning culture
   - a climate for learning
   - teacher as researcher
   - coaching

1 Tweaking

All schools want the same thing: for teachers to constantly seek to improve and develop their practice. Given that the vast majority of teachers are already performing at such a high level, we are talking about making minor adjustments and fine-tuning rather than dramatic changes and a complete overhaul. It is a process that can be referred to as *tweaking*.

The thinking behind the approach is sound:

- people are more likely to make small adjustments than dramatic changes to their practice

- people are more likely to sustain and embed minor adjustments

- the vast majority of teaching is already of a high standard – most teachers therefore do not have the capacity or the need to make dramatic changes to practice.

The starting point of the tweaking process is, of course, identifying where to make the adjustment and deciding upon which bit to tweak. And here we come to the sixty-four-thousand-dollar question:

Who identifies the bit to tweak?

Is this something that is done *to* teachers, or done *by* them? Are teachers adjusting their practice because they have been *told* to, or because they *want* to? If the answer is a combination of the two, where does the emphasis lie?

Simply *telling* teachers what and how to improve may yield some short-term gains, but it will not result in learning.

The way in which schools answer this question is hugely significant and indicative of the prevailing culture and strategic approach to improvement. At one extreme, teachers are making adjustments to their practice because they have been told what and how to tweak; while at the other end of the spectrum, teachers are diagnosing for themselves the way in which they need to adjust their practice.

Both approaches have a place in schools. However, if we aspire to a culture based upon learning, the onus must be on teachers making these decisions for themselves. For simply *telling* teachers what and how to improve may yield some short-term gains but will not result in learning.

> The nature of learning is explored more thoroughly in Section 2. At this point, it is sufficient to suggest that learning:
>
> - is a meaning-making process in which individuals make personal sense of information and experience
>
> - is an active process, done *by* people, not *to* them
>
> - can be enhanced when the process is mediated by another
>
> - best takes place in an atmosphere conducive to risk-taking, collaboration and enquiry
>
> - leads to lasting changes in belief and behaviour.

If these points are accepted, there are some clear implications for schools:

- There is a need to generate information of which to make sense! This in turn makes a strong case that *teachers as researchers* must feature in any professional development programme rooted in learning.

- If learning can be enhanced when mediated by another, there is a powerful argument that *coaching* should play a central role in any professional development programme.

- The internal climate and prevailing culture of the school will create a context that will either enhance or hinder learning.

Reflect

- How do you respond to the list of points above?

- What would you add or amend?

- How would you describe the prevailing culture at your school? To what extent does it enhance or hinder learning?

Cartoon from *A Smile for Monday Morning*, by Phil Suggit and Mike Hughes. See page 256 for details

2 Done *to* / Done *by*

> *No one could be against teachers developing. But there is a critical difference between developing and being developed.*

Martin Holmer

Consider the two scenarios outlined below. In both cases, a group of external consultants had been invited by the school to spend a week observing lessons and to give the staff some feedback at the end. It is interesting to note that when we use the phrase *invited by the school*, we usually mean *invited by the Headteacher*! The staff had simply been informed that the visit would take place and told to turn up at 4.00 pm on the Friday to receive some feedback.

Scenario A

The staff enter the hall slowly and reluctantly after school on Friday. Their body language and general demeanour indicate that most don't want to be there and resent the intrusion into their weekend. A good number of staff keep their coats on.

One of the consultants begins by thanking the staff for staying (the teachers are thinking, *we didn't have a bloody choice*) and delivering a feeble joke (nobody smiles, never mind laughs). The consultant, in time-honoured fashion, then starts by highlighting the positives: ***We were really impressed*** *by the relationships between teachers and students and* ***we thought*** *the way in which learning objectives and learning outcomes were made explicit to students at the beginning of the lesson was excellent* ..., and so on.

This general strategy of highlighting the positives first is, of course, designed to reassure teachers and increase the chances of them being receptive when attention inevitably turns to aspects of the lesson judged to be less impressive and therefore areas for development. Given that one or two teachers nod in agreement – one even smiles – and the body language generally softens, the approach enjoys a degree of success.

Eventually, positives dealt with, attention turns to the less impressive aspects of the lessons. *However,* ***we thought*** *that some of the lessons that we observed lacked challenge* ... At this point, many of the teachers in the room cease to listen – at least, they stop listening properly – as their own internal dialogue dominates their attention. *How dare he ... Who does he think he is ... When was the last time he was in a classroom ... I'd like to see him challenge our kids ... Has he seen the size of the curriculum I've got to cover ...*

The session now becomes a battle; every issue raised by the consultant is challenged (at least internally), every suggestion is countered and for every good reason the consultant can think of to change practice, the teachers can identify ten even better reasons to maintain the status quo.

Judge	Observe
I thought	I noticed
Grade	Non-judgemental data
Feedback	Dialogue
Receive information	Make sense of information
Acceptance/ rejection	Understanding
Compliance	Commitment
Done to	Done by
Leads to dependence	Leads to independence/ inter-dependence

Scenario B

The staff enter the hall slowly and reluctantly after school on Friday. Their body language and general demeanour indicate that most don't want to be there and resent the intrusion into their weekend. A good number of staff keep their coats on.

One of the consultants begins by thanking the staff for staying (the teachers are thinking, *we didn't have a bloody choice*) and delivering a feeble joke (nobody smiles, never mind laughs). Undeterred, he continues, **We noticed** *that about 98% of questions asked by teachers in the classroom are answered correctly first time.*

One of the teachers nods and exclaims, *Oh, that's good!* There is a slight pause before one of her colleagues leans forward and, with a slight frown on her face, poses the question, *Or is it?* There is another slight pause before another teacher adds, *Do you think our questions lack challenge?*

The 'feedback' session continues: *Do you think the kids here are scared to take a risk? ... I wonder if it's the same for all groups ... I'm going to look out for this tomorrow ... What could we do about it?*

Fifty-nine minutes later, the session draws to a close without the consultant having said another word.

I thought / I noticed

These brief vignettes could, of course, be dismissed as a simplistic and idealistic portrayal of an infinitely more complex 'real' world. Maybe there is an element of truth in such an accusation. The events (which actually took place in real schools and with real teachers) are recounted here simply to illustrate two very different approaches to the ultimate goal of improving learning in the classroom.

Scenario A describes an approach essentially based upon *judgements* (clearly illustrated by the frequent use of phrases such as *we thought* and *we were impressed by*) and *feedback*. Inevitably, therefore, it is an approach shrouded in emotion; despite all attempts to highlight the positives first and reassure teachers, human nature ensures that any perceived attack is met with resolute defence. However feedback is dressed up, it is fundamentally a one-way process based upon opinions which will either be accepted or rejected, acted upon or not.

In this example, the assertion that lessons lacked challenge was rejected before it had been considered. **No significant change took place in classrooms.**

Scenario B demonstrates a different approach altogether, based upon *observation* (as illustrated by the phrase *we noticed*) and *professional dialogue*. The very different way in which the same issue was approached generated, not a defensive reaction justifying current practice, but deep reflection, discussion and debate as teachers collectively made sense of the information that had been presented to them and decided how to react to their new understanding.

Significant changes took place in many classrooms as a result of this experience – the catalyst was non-judgemental data.

Done *to* people		Done *by* people
Teaching	⟷	Learning
Monitoring	⟷	Self-evaluation
Feedback	⟷	Dialogue
Training	⟵	Coaching
Extrinsic motivation	⟷	Intrinsic motivation
Compliance	⟷	Commitment
Creates dependency	⟷	Develops capacity
Short-term gains	⟷	Long-term investment

Reflect

Consider the diagram above.

- What colour is your school? (If the answer is *purple*, what shade?)
- What colour would you like it to be?
- How would other people in your school respond to the two questions above?

The approaches adopted in scenarios A and B clearly illustrate the difference between a *done to* and a *done by* culture, as illustrated by the model on the opposite page. As with any model, it is an attempt to make sense of a complex world by simplifying it and it is offered here as no more than food for thought.

Done *to*

In a *done to* culture, the emphasis is on *telling and checking*; teachers tell students, monitor them closely, intervene when necessary and point them in the right direction. Exactly the same thing happens to teachers.

And it works! Clear expectations, explicit guidelines and procedures, feedback to teachers which clearly outlines how to improve, tightly targeted training, and so on, are the basic ingredients for consistently high-quality teaching throughout the school … and good teaching, backed by thorough planning, effective behaviour management systems, tight monitoring of students, early intervention strategies for underachievers, and so on, are the basic ingredients for examination success.

It is undoubtedly an efficient model – if examination and inspection success are the yardstick. However, as was suggested in the introduction:

● Teaching has improved and exam results have risen significantly in recent years. Not surprisingly, the improvements in results have, in many cases, begun to plateau.

For these schools, the challenge now is to build on this success and sustain these improvements. The question to be addressed is whether a *done to*, *tell and check* approach, which may have got us to *good*, is sufficient to move us *beyond good* and break through the plateau.

● The focus has shifted from teaching to learning, and learning involves more than simply telling. It would be somewhat ironic if we simply *told* teachers that it was no longer sufficient to simply *tell* students. Learning is a meaning-making process – for adults, as well as for students.

● While the *done to* approach may yield short-term results, it fails to develop individual capacity, and breeds a *dependency culture*. Students become dependent on the teacher to tell them what to do, how to do it and how well they've done. Similarly, teachers become dependent upon other people telling them how to teach and judging whether or not they have been successful.

● It is an approach that relies heavily upon extrinsic motivation. A heavy enough stick and/or a juicy enough carrot will result in compliance. It should also be noted that extrinsic motivation is subject to an inflationary effect, as rewards and sanctions have to maintain their value in order to be effective. Therefore, if long-term, sustained improvement is going to be driven primarily by extrinsic motivation, sticks will have to become increasingly heavy and carrots ever more juicy to retain their impact.

In your school ...

- What percentage of lesson observations are top-down?

- What percentage of lesson observations are graded?

- Do all teachers have regular opportunities to watch other teachers teach? Do they always observe within their own curriculum area, or can they also watch groups they teach being taught a different subject?

- How regularly to teachers watch *themselves* teach (on video)?

- To what extent is there a systematic swapping of good ideas:

  a) within departments

  b) between departments

  c) between schools?

- How many teachers are currently engaged in some form of action research?

- How much of your professional development programme is done in-house?

- How many teachers are currently coaching?

- How many teachers are currently being coached?

- Where do teachers place Performance Management on the model outlined on page 26? Do they see PM as something that is done *to* them or *by* them?

- How many teachers are engaged in the self-evaluation process – some of them, or all of them?

Done *by*

A shift from a *done to* to a *done by* culture mirrors the way the focus of lessons has switched, with classrooms increasingly dominated by learning, self-assessment and learning to learn. These are essentially *done by* activities, the role of the teacher evolving from simply telling students, to helping them make sense. It does not mean that students are never told, corrected or guided – simply that the emphasis has changed.

However, the move towards a *done by* approach has not always extended to teachers. Indeed, the understandable response of many schools to an OFSTED regime now firmly rooted in self-evaluation has been to increase monitoring! It would appear that the SEF is an insatiable beast; inspection may have switched from external to internal, but from the teacher's perspective it is something that is still being done *to* them. Not surprisingly, many are defensive.

Learning is done *by* people. If schools truly wish to be 'learning schools', then teachers must be learners too and the entire culture must be based upon a *done by* approach. That is not to say that teachers are never monitored, never receive feedback or never attend training. It simply means that **the emphasis switches from monitoring, feedback and training to reflection, dialogue and coaching**.

Such an approach seeks more than immediate results. Rather, a *done by* culture seeks to develop the capacity of each individual to reflect, learn and act with increasing independence. As such, it is a longer-term investment that pursues sustainable improvement over a period of time rather than quick-fixes.

Both are important

On page 27, it was suggested that the 'red', *done to*, approach works – at least, to a certain extent. Many would go further than this and suggest that the 'red' side of the *done to/done by* spectrum shown on page 26 – an element of monitoring and instruction – is also *necessary* at both classroom and whole-school level.

There is a valid argument that the real world demands an element of 'red', not least because the 'red' side of the spectrum generates the information that is required by the SEF. It should also be acknowledged that the SEF is not an end in itself; it is the SEF that both informs and drives strategic planning.

There is also a compelling argument that a key element of effective leadership is flexibility. Different situations require different leadership styles and a characteristic of effective teachers and Headteachers is the ability to move between both sides of the spectrum, selecting the appropriate approach for the particular occasion and set of circumstances. There are times when Headteachers need to decide and direct; there are times when teachers need to tell and instruct.

It is therefore important to acknowledge that **being 'red' is *not* a problem; relying exclusively on 'red' *is*.**

Is risk-taking in your school:

- frowned upon?
- tolerated?
- encouraged?
- expected?

How would the rest of the staff respond?

Done *with*

The diagram on page 26 is no more than a model and presents two extreme ends of a spectrum. Reality is rarely black and white – or in this case red and blue. There is clearly some middle ground here – which could possibly be described as a *done with* approach. However, schools that claim to be somewhere between *done to* and *done by* are rarely exactly half-way between the two extremes, and tend to favour one side or the other. The culture within a school is therefore essentially a matter of *emphasis* and it is apparent that this differs significantly between schools.

3 The learning culture

This book is based upon the premise that long-term, sustainable improvement must be facilitated, rather than driven, and firmly rooted in learning.

Three elements of such a culture are highlighted in this section:
- a climate conducive to learning
- the role of teacher as researcher
- coaching.

A climate for learning

Few would dispute that learning flourishes in an environment in which people are encouraged to be reflective and self-critical, take risks, try out new strategies and approaches, learn together, support each other, challenge and be challenged. If this is true, then these are precisely the conditions that we must strive to create, not only for students but for teachers.

It can be argued that the national context actually militates against risk-taking and that the highly pressurised environment created by central policy has actually bred suspicion, competition and a need to be on the defensive against the perceived threat. Justification, rather than reflection, is for many schools and teachers the order of the day. People are so busy looking over their shoulders that they understandably forget to look forward.

These are hardly the conditions in which learning flourishes. However, the good news is that many schools have successfully created a culture of professional reflection despite government policy. Indeed, the unfavourable conditions nationally make it even more important that school leaders use their influence where they can and create an internal climate conducive to learning and risk-taking.

Differences between schools, however slight, are hugely significant, for it is these differences that both:

- **reflect the culture**

- **contribute to it.**

Cultures are created

Although every school is unique, there are certain factors and experiences that are common to all – for example, OFSTED, PANDAS, Performance Management, League Tables and the fact that there are only twenty four hours in a day. It is always of interest, therefore, if a school claims that something *can't be done because there isn't time* or *because of OFSTED,* when other schools manage to do it.

In addition, there is a national dimension to education these days as never before; we have a National Curriculum, National Strategies, a National Leadership College, and so on. Not surprisingly then, there are huge similarities between schools and classrooms. Watch a Y2 literacy lesson in Newcastle and another in Cornwall and it may well be only the accents that are different.

However, all schools and classrooms, while broadly similar, are also different. These differences are often slight and subtle and, unless you are looking for them, easily missed. Indeed, the differences are so small it is easy to dismiss or underestimate them. This would be a huge mistake, as the differences are highly significant.

These differences in approach are more than revealing indicators of the prevailing culture; they contribute to it. For cultures do not just exist, they are created – consciously or otherwise. Every word, action, procedure and policy – however small and seemingly insignificant – is, on a continual basis, simultaneously reflecting and creating the context in which teachers work. When they are considered in isolation, it is tempting to dismiss these differences as inconsequential; however, when added together they exert a subtle yet powerful influence on the mindset of teachers.

It is the Headteacher and senior staff who exert the most influence on the internal climate of the school. Every word and deed is a message that is received and interpreted by individual teachers – usually at a sub-conscious level – and it is the combined perceptions of teachers over a period of time that go a long way to determining whether the environment encourages and permits teachers to think and act like learners.

If, in crude terms, everything we do and say in school will make it more or less likely that teachers will be prepared to be learners, three things are worth bearing in mind:

1   Messages must be consistent over time.

2   Words and deeds must be congruent.

3   Small, seemingly innocuous incidents can have a significant effect on perception.

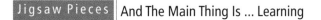
Ruth Butler contends that:

Giving grades as feedback can undermine motivation: pre-occupation with grade attainment can lower the quality of the performance.

It is one of the reasons behind the significant shift in emphasis when assessing children, from assessment of learning to assessment for and assessment as learning.

Carol Dweck identifies two main kinds of motivation:

1 learning orientation

2 performance orientation.

Those with a learning orientation:

- have a belief in their ability to improve and learn
- have a preference for challenging tasks
- derive satisfaction from personal success at difficult tasks.

Those with a performance orientation:

- have a concern to be judged as able to perform
- derive satisfaction from doing better than others
- place an emphasis on normative public evaluation.

Crucially, those with a learning orientation have a concern for **improving** their competence while those with a performance orientation are concerned with **proving** their competence.

Reflect

- Does this just apply to children?
- Are the teachers in your school concerned with improving or proving their competence?
- A summary of Carol Dweck's work can be found in Pedagogy and Practice, Unit 9, DfES (2004). See page 252 for details.

Teacher as researcher

The very mention of the word 'research' deters some teachers, for they equate research with high-brow, jargon-ridden academic documents that paint a picture of the classroom bearing little resemblance to the world that they themselves inhabit. And yet, research comes in all shapes and sizes and from a wide variety of sources. It may indeed be formal academic research. Equally, it may well comprise small-scale investigations into a single aspect of teaching and learning, which many people would quite probably not even refer to as research. Both have their place and can come from external sources or can be generated from within the school.

All that we are seeking to do is:

1 generate useful information that can inform both policy and practice
2 deepen our understanding of learning – for the more we understand about learning, the better able we are to facilitate it in others.

These twin aims demand that teachers are involved in some form of research, for – while external sources can provide information to satisfy the first point – if the purpose of research is indeed to deepen our understanding of learning, then teachers have to be involved in the process.

Non-judgemental data

Non-judgemental data is the key to establishing a culture of professional reflection and dialogue. It can also be the catalyst to genuine, sustainable improvements in the classroom. Consider the following:

● We are seeking to create an environment conducive to professional reflection.
● Emotion is a barrier to reflection.
● Judgements generate an emotional response.
● Judgements therefore militate against deep personal reflection.
● In many schools, teachers are being judged on a regular basis.

Schools are awash with data these days. However, often it is judgement-based and reflects performance and attainment. While much of it is both necessary and helpful, it is important to remember that data derived from judgement is often personal and a little too close to home to prompt meaningful reflection. Myles Downey in his book *Effective Coaching* argues that:

> *... the issue of distance is important in coaching. If a coachee is caught up in a difficult or emotional topic, there is no distance and this almost creates the problem.*

(The whole issue of coaching is considered in more detail on pages 47–63.)

How many of the following can you answer?

1   What percentage of lessons in your school are judged to be satisfactory or better?

2   What percentage of lessons in your school are judged to be excellent?

3   What is the percentage of questions answered correctly first time by students?

4   When, on average, does the first open question appear in lessons?

5   What is the balance between teacher-talk and learner-talk in your lessons?

6   What is the balance between questions generated by the teacher and questions generated by the students in your lessons?

7   What is the balance between open and closed questions asked by teachers in the classroom?

8   What is the average length of time that a teacher waits *after* a student has given an answer before they begin to talk?

9   How many times was Jonathon in Year 8 addressed by his first name last week?

10 How many teachers congratulated Amanda when she passed her Grade One violin exam?

Reality–perception gap

There is a second compelling argument for generating non-judgemental data: what teachers *think* is happening in the classroom and what is *actually* taking place can often be two quite separate things! In particular, teachers often underestimate how much they talk. Any decision to make a change to practice should be based upon precisely what is happening, yet there is often a difference – sometimes a significant difference – between perception and reality.

Consider questions 3 to 10 on the opposite page. How many teachers could answer these questions accurately? Most teachers have either never consciously considered these issues or can only respond in a general way – *I think it's about ...*

Establishing reality

At the risk of being contentious, one might tentatively suggest that while many schools know precisely how well lessons are being taught, fewer schools know precisely what is taking place in the classroom! All schools can answer questions 1 and 2 on the opposite page – most schools can only guess at 3 to 10.

Establishing precisely what is happening is the starting point for developing classroom practice. Establishing reality is also a key feature of the coaching process, for coaching essentially involves helping people determine:

- where they are
- where they would like to be
- how they are going to get there.

The GROW model

The need to establish what is happening is made explicit in the GROW model – a standard coaching template that was first developed by Sir John Whitmore and is just beginning to find its way into schools.

G establish the **GOAL**	consider where you would like to be
R establish **REALITY**	consider what is happening now
O establish the **OPTIONS**	consider what could be done
W establish **WHAT NEXT?**	decide on a future course of action

Using tools to establish reality

- The tools described in this book, and listed opposite, are not designed for formal academic research. Most do not produce objective data. This is deliberate; a key aim of these tools is to generate discussion, disagreement and deep reflection and so satisfy points 1–4 opposite.

- The tools can be used flexibly. For example, many suggest that you take a sounding every 15 seconds. The procedure will work equally well with time segments of 30 seconds, 1 minute and so on. Similarly, some tools require a sounding after 15, 30 and 45 minutes. This assumes a 60 minutes lesson and should be adjusted accordingly. Use them in whatever way works for you.

- Some tools require children to record their thoughts; this should be done anonymously. It can be helpful, however, to ask each child to state his or her sex on the form so that any differences in perception between boys and girls can be identified.

- We have to accept that some children or groups may not respond in a totally sensible manner! It is therefore important to manage this process properly. It is obviously tempting to only use these tools with the 'right children'. We must be aware, however, that this may skew the results – sometimes significantly.

- Using the tool just once will give you a single snapshot. This may be of some interest but will arguably be of limited value. Use the tool over a period of time, with different groups, and so on. What trends emerge? What do these tell you about your teaching and the way in which students perceive your lessons?

- The most effective tools are often the ones that you have designed yourself. The key point is that if we are looking for different things, we need to look through different eyes.

Coaching is rooted in learning, and learning involves making meaning – making personal sense of information and experience. If we subscribe to the principle that teachers need to be learners, then clearly they require information to make sense of – in other words, data. When a teacher becomes aware that 90% of the questions she asks a top set are answered correctly first time, compared to a corresponding figure of 20% when teaching a bottom set, or that on average the first open question in her lessons is posed after 12 minutes, she has information to reflect upon. She now knows where she is, and can begin to think through where she would like to be, and how she is going to get there. She could of course do this alone – or the process could be mediated by another.

Different tools

If the aim of the exercise is to generate information that will …

1   accurately portray what is happening in the classroom

2   stimulate professional reflection and dialogue

3   inform the coaching process

4   help us deepen our understanding of learning

… it is clear that the standard observation sheets built around the OFSTED judgemental model will not suffice. For we are not looking to make judgements; we are seeking to generate the information that will in turn provide the catalyst for points **1–4** above.

If we seek different kinds of data, it follows that we need different kinds of tools to help us find it. The following tools are currently being used in schools across the country.

Summary of the reflective tools described in this book

- The Zone of Challenge   pages 40 and 140
- Dissecting a lesson   page 86
- Assessing the teaching–learning balance   page 108
- The TIMS grid   page 112
- Capturing the structure of a lesson   page 122
- Intrinsic and extrinsic motivation   page 128
- How challenged are you?   page 138
- The Curiosity Indicator   page 214
- Which best describes your classroom?   pages 76 and 204
- Diamond Nine   page 166

The Zone of Challenge

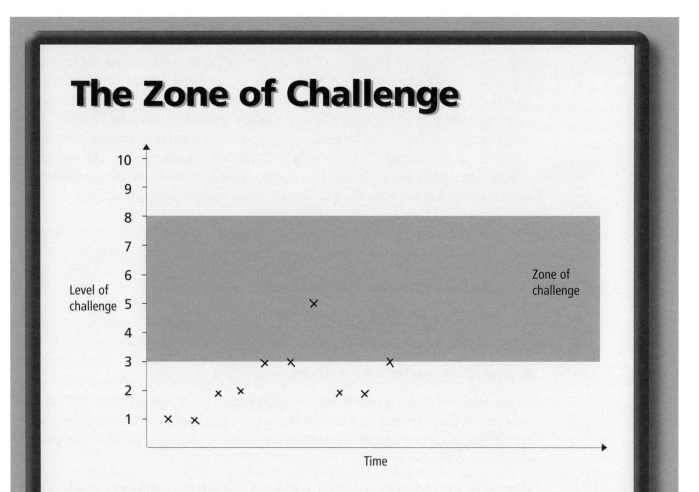

Procedure:

On a scale of 1–10, consider the level of challenge for students, during every 30-second interval throughout the lesson (or larger intervals if you prefer). Record your feelings on the axes as shown above.

The scale:

Use 1–3 when you consider the activities to be too easy, and 8–10 when tasks are too difficult. (The intention is not to put a 'glass ceiling' on learning, but simply to acknowledge that people cannot learn too far in advance of their current level of understanding.) Thus there is a *zone of challenge* (between 3 and 8, shaded above) in which children are being stretched and challenged without finding the work impossibly difficult.

Vygotsky would have referred to this as the Zone of Proximal Development.

Example: *From gathering data to changes in practice*

The following example took place in a real school, the focus for the work being the level of challenge that children faced in the classroom. There was unanimous agreement that getting the level of challenge right was a key to successful learning – when things are too easy, children become bored and restless; when things are too hard, they give up and switch off. The teachers agreed that they were aiming for lessons that were challenging, interesting and engaging – but not impossible. This was their **GOAL**.

In order to build up an accurate picture of what was currently taking place during lessons – or establish **REALITY** – staff used a 'zone of challenge' graph such as that shown opposite during peer observations or when reflecting on their own video-recorded lessons. Over some weeks, many graphs were completed from a variety of curriculum areas, and when the staff sat down to unpick the information, a remarkably consistent picture emerged. On average, between 10 and 13 minutes of each lesson elapsed before students were really being challenged and engaged. (The graph opposite is representative of what was actually found.)

For example, one History lesson had begun with a series of anagrams on the board. Most people would accept that, when the focus of the unit of work is NAZI Germany, deciphering ZANI is not the most challenging of starts. LERHIT is only slightly more difficult!

Many lessons had begun with children copying down learning objectives and writing down their homework task, followed by a series of low-level, closed questions to recap on the previous lesson. Sharing learning objectives with students and setting homework early in the lesson are generally considered to be good practice and beginning a lesson in this way would almost certainly get a tick in the OFSTED box. However, when the same scenario is viewed through different eyes we simply see children *copying*. Not that challenging.

Reflecting on this information, teachers quickly concluded that there was a gap between what they wanted to see happening – that is, students being challenged (**GOAL**) – and what was actually taking place in the lessons (**REALITY**). It must be stressed at this point that nobody is questioning the wisdom of ensuring that students understand precisely what they are going to be learning. However, the inescapable conclusion was that many lesson starts were slow, similar and failed to challenge students and capture their imagination immediately they walked through the door.

The discussion moved on to what might be done differently in order to get students in the *zone of challenge* earlier in the lesson. Various ideas were suggested as the group considered their **OPTIONS** and decided on **WHAT NEXT.** It had been noted during the earlier discussion that it was often the first *open question* that really engaged and challenged the children, and it was decided therefore to frame learning experiences in the form of an open question and to ensure that higher level questions appeared much earlier in the proceedings. One teacher employed and egg timer and set herself the personal target of asking an open question before the sand ran out!

Returning to the History classroom described above, we now find a teacher at the doorway greeting students in German. The children raised an eyebrow and enquired if the teacher was alright, to which she replied, *I'm fine thank you; I'm just wondering if we'd all be talking German now if Hitler had invaded immediately after Dunkirk? That's what we are thinking about today and by the end of the lesson you will all be able to express an opinion and justify the thinking behind it.* The discussion had begun before the students had even sat down.

Example: Arbourthorne Primary School, Sheffield – *using video to reflect on lessons*

Kate Battersby, SENCO

Context

- 3–11 Primary School
- NOR 408

Following school Inset with Mike Hughes, Arbourthorne Primary School adopted the four-phase model (see Section 3, page 81) as a basis for planning lessons and a framework for Performance Management lesson observations. Perhaps more importantly, it provided a structured and systematic approach to improving the quality of our teaching and learning by enabling us to focus upon specific aspects of our lessons in turn.

We reflected upon and discussed the four phases of our lessons and it was agreed that the fourth phase (reflect and review) was too frequently squeezed out or rushed through and that this aspect of teaching and learning would be an ideal place to do some tweaking.

To encourage realistic self-reflection, we decided to video the ends of our lessons. We had employed this technique before during an action research project which had aimed to assess and improve speaking and listening opportunities. This process had revealed that, despite our confidence that we were offering children a high number of quality speaking and listening opportunities, the reality was quite different. Many of us were shocked by the findings and vowed to make changes. A follow-up study revealed that once teachers had become more self-aware, we were quickly able to make significant changes to our practice which in turn had a positive impact on the quality of our teaching and learning.

Staff watched the video clips together and reflected on what they had seen: *What is actually taking place? What works? What doesn't? How can we improve?* This process was strengthened by a series of peer observations, which gave us all a chance to watch our colleagues in action. We learned much from the process and were able to identify strategies and techniques which could benefit our own teaching. Working with peers in this way proved highly supportive and far less intimidating than senior management observations. Teachers were much more likely to move out of their comfort zone!

Following our initial video-recording, we continued with self-reflection and peer observations for a high-intensity half term, which ended with another videoed review. This process supported us in tweaking the way in which our lessons ended and helped to further cement professional reflection into our school culture.

The use of video

If our ultimate aim is to help teachers make sense of what is taking place in the classroom in order to further develop their practice, there is a persuasive argument that all teachers should be able to watch themselves teach on video on a regular basis.

Yet this is an area in which practice between schools varies considerably. In some schools, teachers have never seen themselves teach while in others watching yourself teach is regarded as nothing less than an entitlement and considered to be a key strategy in encouraging teachers to reflect on their practice.

The thinking behind the approach is sound; people are far more likely to make a change when they both *want* to and accept the *need* to. This is in stark contrast to expecting teachers to adjust their practice because they have been *told* to. You can tell someone something until you are blue in the face but sometimes they will only accept it when they have seen it for themselves.

Most teachers are understandably reticent about watching themselves on video. However, while few teachers claim to enjoy the experience, you would be hard pushed to find anyone who didn't find the experience valuable. Most significantly, practice often changes as a result.

While there are clearly many ways to organise the video-recording of lessons, there would appear to be two golden rules:

1   Teachers have to buy into the process. Reflection of this nature is essentially a *done by* process; it is contradictory to make people do it.

2   The recording is the property of the individual teacher. He or she decides who, if anyone, gets to see the lesson. This process is about professional development, rather than monitoring.

While simply video-recording a lesson and watching yourself teach can be a powerful and significant moment, the process becomes potentially far more powerful when two or more teachers can watch together. Again, this is a matter of choice and cannot be imposed; the teacher who taught the lesson decides whether or not to share the video and with whom. The purpose of the exercise is *not* to judge the lesson but to promote discussion and reflection.

For example, two or more teachers complete the exercise on page 108. They do this independently and then compare graphs. The areas of disagreement are of particular interest – in simple terms, when one person has drawn a mostly red bar for a particular five-minute period, and another has drawn a mostly blue bar. Neither is right or wrong, but the different interpretation of the same events will inevitably be a catalyst for professional dialogue ... and **it is professional dialogue that lies at the heart of professional reflection**.

Example: Somervale School, Midsomer Norton – *professional enquiry teams*

Mark Kenny, Deputy Headteacher

Context

● 11–18 Secondary School – Media Arts College specialising in English, Music and Media.

● NOR 800

● now judged a rapidly improving school, having come out of special measures in May 2005

● stated vision of becoming a *'coaching school'* where the *'art of teaching meets the science of learning'*

The idea of establishing professional enquiry teams, while simultaneously offering volunteers the chance to train as coaches, had been floating around the school for a few years. The catalyst that turned this idea into reality was the DfES *Pedagogy and Practice (PED) Packs*, which offer an Action Research Model for improving professional practice. This coincided with a pilot project in which six staff were trained to be coaches. The question was then how to train twelve more staff as coaches without significant internal disruption. The decision was therefore taken to amalgamate work on the PED packs with further coaching training and incorporate this package into the existing five Inset days.

Procedure

● Four leading practitioners were identified to lead a *Teaching and Learning Enquiry Group* based around a specific PED pack. The Lead Practitioner for each group was responsible for setting the pace and monitoring the work of the group.

● PED packs chosen for the focus of the Enquiry Groups were: 1) Active Engagement Techniques, 2) Leading in Learning and Questioning Skills, 3) Preparing Lessons for the Less Able and Teaching and Learning Styles, and 4) ICT Across the Curriculum.

● As part of the school's review of teaching and learning, a new meeting was set up in school known as the Teaching and Learning Forum, where new ideas on teaching were showcased and traded. This was used to outline each of the PED packs and the coaching training on offer.

● Each member of staff chose which Enquiry Group they wished to join or whether they wished to train as coaches. The only restriction was that each curriculum area should ensure that they were represented across a range of groups.

● Two Inset days – October 2005 and February 2006 – were dedicated to work within the groups. In addition, the groups met in the times designated for the Teaching and Learning Forum six times a year to review progress and plan future action. During this time, a parallel group of staff underwent coaching training.

● One Inset day was collapsed in order to create time for peer observation. The expectation was that five hours would be spent by the group watching colleagues teach, feeding back on the enquiry issue and so on. The initial collapsing of an Inset day was a significant factor in helping staff to commit to the process.

● Each group was given one academic year to work through the suggested activities contained in the PED pack and complete a series of lesson observations. By the end of the year all members of the enquiry group had observed each other teaching on five separate occasions. During these lessons, ideas contained in the PED packs were trialled. All teachers received feedback at the end of the lesson.

For example, an NVQ teacher, the Head of English and an ICT teacher joint-planned a lesson using the inductive model as outlined in the PED Pack 3 as a template for lesson design.

● Enquiry teams reported back to the entire staff during the last meeting of the year.

By the end of the year, each teacher:

● had trialled a new way of working

● had been observed by a colleague and received feedback on the new way of working

● had observed colleagues trialling a new way of working and given them feedback

● had begun working on embedding the new way of working into their daily practice.

Although it is impossible to isolate the impact of a single strategy, it is appropriate to point out that interviews with students reveal a marked increase in engagement and significant improvement in their enjoyment of lessons since 2004.

In quantitative terms:

● Examination results as measured by 5A*–C grades rose by 17% in 2005. They are predicted to rise by a further 10% in 2006.

● In 2004, OFSTED judged teaching in core subjects to be unsatisfactory. By May 2005 OFSTED judged over 70% of lessons to be good or better.

● By May 2006, internal self-evaluation measures showed teaching to be good or better in 75% of lessons and satisfactory or better in 96% of lessons.

> *Planning lessons with colleagues from other curriculum areas and receiving feedback from these colleagues on how the lesson could be improved was one of the most professionally rewarding things I have ever done.*

Leader of PED Pack Group

It is possible to argue that, without coaching and reflection, learning cannot in fact take place.

John West-Burnham

Coaching

 Coaching by definition encourages learning.

Myles Downey

Coaching is currently everywhere; there are books, courses and column-inch after column-inch devoted to it in the TES and other educational publications. It rather makes you wonder how we managed without it for so long, for although a handful of schools were committed to coaching as a vehicle for personal and professional growth more than a decade ago, they were certainly in a minority. For the majority of the profession, coaching is very much the new kid on the block.

Indeed, coaching has come a long way in a very short period of time and, although still undoubtedly in its infancy in schools, it is likely to develop at an even faster rate in the foreseeable future. It remains to be seen, however, precisely which direction developments will take, for coaching means different things to different people and – in common with learning – lacks a single, universally accepted definition.

This lack of clarity needs to be resolved – and quickly – if coaching is to realise its undoubted potential and transform the way in which many schools operate. For learning lies at the heart of coaching and if we are genuinely seeking to create organisations truly based on learning, in which teachers are learners too, it is clear that coaching can play a powerful role. Indeed, it may be possible to go further and suggest – as John West-Burnham asserts, opposite – that coaching is a prerequisite for schools committed to putting learning centre-stage.

However:

- Much currently takes place under the umbrella label of 'coaching', and it is clear that there is considerable variation in practice between schools.

- Many people interpret coaching as a series of events – usually a pre-lesson chat, a lesson observation and a subsequent feedback and coaching session. At best this is an extremely limited interpretation of coaching; at worst it isn't actually coaching at all.

- Few teachers have extensive coaching experience. What teachers often possess is considerable experience of *mentoring* – and coaching and mentoring are different animals.

- There are therefore significant implications for the way in which the world of education develops coaching skills – or coaches the coaches. Yet many of the people currently providing coaching training have themselves only limited experience of both coaching and developing coaching skills in others.

Coaching is a non-judgemental process – this core principle runs through coaching like BLACKPOOL runs through a stick of sea-side rock.

A comprehensive coverage of coaching and related issues is beyond the scope of this particular book (Coaching in Schools by Mike Hughes deals with this theme in detail – see page 254). However, it is appropriate to expand a little on the points made on page 47.

Let us begin by examining the nature of coaching.

- **Coaching is a non-judgemental process.** This core principle runs through coaching like BLACKPOOL runs through a stick of sea-side rock, and is the feature that distinguishes coaching from other forms of professional development.

- **The person being coached (the coachee) is in control of the agenda.** Indeed, it is their agenda – the role of the coach, to paraphrase Laura Whitworth, is to make sure that their agenda doesn't get lost.

- **The coach's job is to help people think through their issues.** Their role is to listen, reflect back and ask questions, rather than provide answers and give advice. Sir John Whitmore, in his highly recommended book *Coaching for Performance*, describes coaching as *unlocking a person's potential to maximise their own performance. It is helping them learn rather than teaching them.*

The non-judgemental dimension is critical. Research suggests that coaching works – in other words, it leads to lasting change and improvements in performance – where other more traditional forms of professional development fail. Indeed, it is the overwhelming nature of this evidence that is arguably the reason for such an emphasis on coaching at a national level. It should, of course, come as no surprise that people move on when they both want to and accept the need to, rather than because somebody else has told them to.

And here we come to the crucial point: coaching works because of what it is – because of the precise make-up and characteristics of its particular approach. Central to this is the non-judgemental nature, which in many respects is the core distinctive ingredient of the coaching dish. In a similar way, pasta is central to lasagne. You can cook lasagne with or without mushrooms and it remains fundamentally lasagne. However, if you replace pasta with mashed potato you end up with shepherd's pie – a completely different dish. Certainly, there are similarities between shepherd's pie and lasagne – and there are times when shepherd's pie hits the spot – but, they are fundamentally different.

Take away the non-judgemental element of coaching and you take away the central ingredient – you end up with a completely different dish. It may look like coaching but if it comes with judgements – however subtle – it quite simply isn't.

Much of what is currently taking place under the coaching label isn't actually coaching. It may look like coaching, it may even be called coaching, but if it comes with judgements, however subtle and however well camouflaged, it quite simply isn't.

Coaching as camouflage

Much of what is currently taking place in schools under the coaching umbrella is, when examined closely, fundamentally judgemental. For example:

- Coaching in schools frequently has a hierarchical dimension to it. Line Managers are increasingly asked to play a coaching role. Not surprisingly, many teachers are suspicious that coaching is therefore a trendy new label for monitoring.

- If not line managers, excellent teachers – with or without formal Advanced Skills (AST) status – are acting as teaching and learning coaches in schools. They have been selected for their undoubted excellence in the classroom, rather than for their coaching potential. This is not to suggest that excellent teachers cannot also be effective coaches – although many coaching experts claim that the better you know a subject, the harder it is to be non-judgemental and act in a detached coaching capacity – simply that in many cases the whole approach to coaching is predicated on judgement. It is understandable, therefore, when coaching is perceived as something done *by* the good teachers, *to* the weaker ones.

- Many 'coaching' sessions begin with the coach asking the teacher what they thought of the lesson. It is ironic that this ostensibly non-judgemental process so often begins by the coach inviting a judgement! Having then listened to the teacher's perception of the lesson, the coach responds by asking a few questions and making a series of suggestions. However, the nature of these questions is significant for questions that begin with phrases such as, *Don't you think that … Isn't it the case that … Have you thought of …* and the classic, *If you could do your plenary again, how might you do it differently?* aren't really questions at all; they are statements. What is more, they are statements that are clearly designed to help the teacher arrive at the 'right' answer, or, in other words, reach the judgement that the coach has already made.

When the above conditions prevail, the label 'coaching' is being used to camouflage the fact that judgements are being made and teachers are being told how to improve – or at least guided in particular directions. It may look like coaching, it may even be called coaching, but **if it is based upon judgements, however subtle and however well hidden, it isn't coaching**. Coaching is more than a change of label; coaching represents a fundamental change of emphasis.

Reflect

Is the 'coaching' that is taking place in your school:

- non-judgemental
- not overtly judgemental?

Part of the culture

Picture the scene. It is lesson change-over in a large secondary school and, as is typical, a large number of people are moving quickly in a confined area.

A teacher, who was hurrying to her next lesson, passed two sixth-form students in the corridor and one asked, *Excuse me Miss, have you got a minute? I've been thinking; which university do you think I should go to?*

Her reply was instantaneous: *What do you want to get out of your university experience? Where do you want to be in five years? Where do you want to be in ten years?*

The student muttered, *Thanks Miss*, before turning away deep in thought.

The teacher reflected on the incident afterwards:

We don't even call it coaching anymore. It's just become the way we talk with each other – in the classroom, in the corridor, on the playground, in the staffroom. Our first thought is not to tell people what we think they should do but help them think things through for themselves. It's just part of the culture here.

Event or philosophy?

Many people in the world of education equate coaching with a lesson observation sandwiched between a pre- and post-observation conversation. Some people even refer to this as *the* coaching cycle.

This, however, is an extremely limited view of coaching akin to interpreting breakfast as a bowl of cornflakes. Cornflakes are just one possibility; so too a planning, observation and feedback cycle. When coaching is perceived in such a narrow way, it is in danger of being reduced to an *event* – something that takes place in private, between two consenting adults lasting approximately thirty minutes. Yet coaching is potentially so much more than an event; coaching is a *philosophy*.

Coaching is about helping people help themselves, and is based on the unshakable belief that the power to change comes from within. It is not about telling and guiding, it is about holding up a mirror and posing the questions in order to help people think through issues. Sir John Whitmore puts it in a nutshell when he says that coaching people is about *helping them learn rather than teaching them.*

Coaching is, therefore, a set of beliefs and a way of working – it would not be over-dramatic to describe it as *a way of life* – that essentially describe the way in which people relate to each other. Although it is a word that is frequently used to describe a professional development activity, a leadership style and an approach to teaching, coaching is a concept that is not confined to formal settings. **Coaching is an 'anytime, anyplace, anywhere' philosophy** and is just as likely to surface in the corridor (see opposite) or on the playground as it is in an office. Nor is it the preserve of adults; children can coach and be coached – coaching is simply a way of behaving and believing.

When coaching is viewed in this way, it is clear that to limit it to an event would be to miss a trick; coaching has the potential to permeate an entire institution and influence the culture. More than that, coaching has the potential to *be* the culture; and if coaching is inextricably linked to learning …

Coaching or mentoring?

Many people confuse coaching with mentoring. This is not surprising as for many years it was common-place within the education world to use the terms interchangeably. However, while they may be related, coaching and mentoring are fundamentally different.

In crude terms, mentoring is about teaching while coaching is rooted firmly in learning. Mentors generally have greater expertise than the person they are working with and their role is to pass on tips and advice and generally guide. Essentially, and at the risk of being over-simplistic, mentors *tell*. Coaching on the other hand is not dependent upon the coach having greater experience or expertise than the coachee – NQTs can coach Headteachers – as their job is to listen, reflect back and help people think through their issues. In a nutshell, coaches help people make sense – coaches *help people learn.*

Coaching has the potential to *be* the culture, and if coaching is inextricably linked to learning ...

What many schools have in place is some form of mentoring system. This is not surprising, as a great many schools – while sympathetic to the aspirations on page 57 – have as their immediate priority the need to improve next year's examination results. This necessitates improving the quality of teaching in the classroom and the quickest way of doing that is to tap into internal expertise and to create systems and structures that enable the strongest teachers to pass on tips and advice to their less effective colleagues.

Mentoring has a role to play

It is important to stress here that mentoring is an effective, necessary and, at times, appropriate form of professional development. There are times when you just need to tell and be told – they are times when you just need to know. There are also a great many teachers out there with enormous professional expertise and it makes perfect sense for their pearls of wisdom be shared with others. There is no suggestion otherwise, nor is there a claim that coaching is the answer for everyone and every issue.

The key message here is that coaching and mentoring are *different*. Both have much to offer. The problem arises when the two are confused and schools think they are implementing a coaching programme when in fact a version of mentoring is taking place.

Ask Why, not What

Many people are asking *What is coaching?* The pertinent question, however, may well be, *Why coaching?* James Flaherty in *Coaching: Evoking Excellence in Others* suggests that the *what* and the *why* cannot be divorced. In other words, we must be crystal clear about what we hope to achieve by coaching in order to help shape precisely what it is.

If you are seeking to ...

- find a quick-fix solution
- improve next year's examination results
- improve teachers (as opposed to help teachers improve)
- exploit the expertise of your most effective teachers by giving them a chance to pass on tips and advice to weaker members of staff

... then it is highly doubtful that coaching is the appropriate vehicle, for the above motives are more likely to be achieved by a strategy based upon monitoring and mentoring. Similarly, if you are contemplating coaching solely because the DfES et al are encouraging it and everyone else seems to be doing it, it is unlikely that the approach will truly take root and flourish.

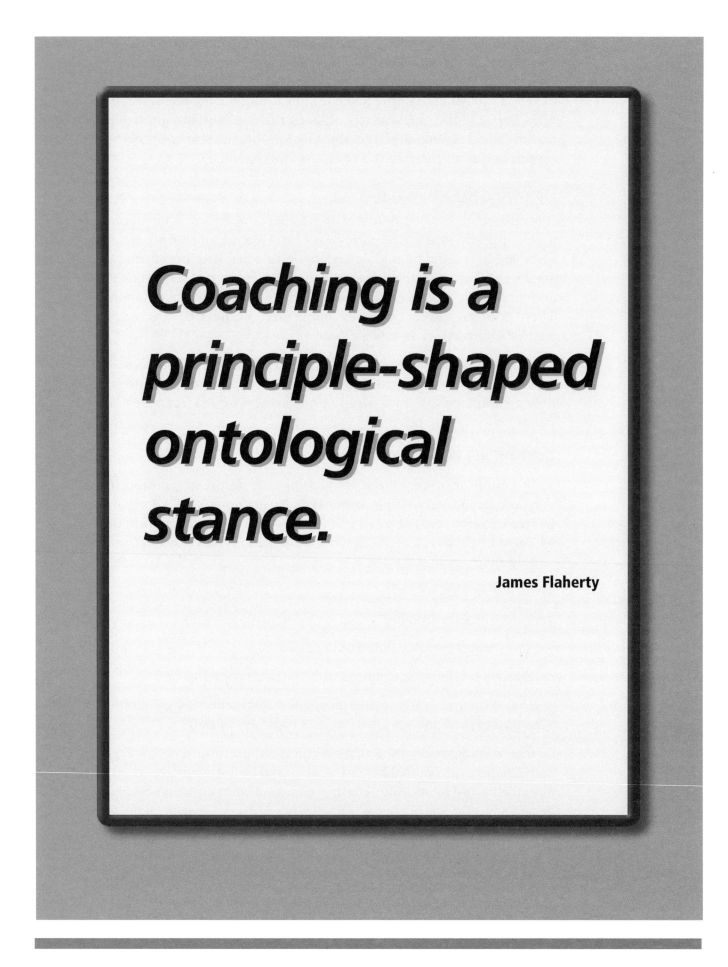

Coaching is a principle-shaped ontological stance.

James Flaherty

However, if you are seeking ...

- to empower the individual
- to develop individual capacity
- to help teachers help themselves
- intrinsically motivated teachers
- teachers as learners
- long-term, sustainable improvement
- a culture of professional reflection

... then coaching may be the vehicle for you.

James Flaherty suggests that the *products of coaching* are:

- long-term excellence
- self-correction
- self-generation.

If these, and the list above, are the aspirations, then it is clear that coaching must be much more than skilful practitioners telling colleagues with less expertise how to teach – however subtly and tactfully that is done.

Reflect

- How do you respond to the reasons for coaching above?

- What would you wish to add to this list?

- How do these motives compare with your reasons for introducing coaching in your school?

- What do you hope to achieve in the short term and in the long term?

- Is your interpretation of coaching compatible with your motives for introducing it?

- Are you currently coaching or mentoring (or both)?

- Is everyone in the school clear about the difference between coaching and mentoring?

- Is every member of staff clear about the reasons for introducing coaching in the school – are they clear about the *why*?

Example: Warwickshire Inclusion Network – *variations on the coaching theme*

Colin Bradley, Co-Leader, Warwickshire Inclusion Network

Context

● Warwickshire Inclusion Network (WIN) consists of six secondary schools, four primary schools and two special schools.

● Middle and senior school leaders from schools across the network took part in a series of workshops designed to develop coaching skills, as part of a wider leadership development programme.

Outcomes

The outcomes of the programme included significant and hugely varied developments in a number of schools:

● A scheme – *The Learning Challenge Coaching Programme* – was introduced in which Year 10 students were given coaching training and then acted as coaches to Year 9 students. The following year, the Year 9 students who had been coached became the coaches.

● A number of teachers employed coaching style techniques when working with individual students. For example, a science teacher used the GROW model (see page 37) with a Year 11 student who had been experiencing some difficulties, to help him organise his approach to revision more effectively.

● A Head of Faculty initiated a scheme in which teachers were paired together to both coach and be coached. They received coaching training and were introduced to the GROW model before being given some time to observe lessons and coach each other. Some pairs went on to team teach. Results in the Faculty have shown a significant improvement.

● A coaching approach was adopted to conduct Performance Management interviews in one of the Network's Primary Schools.

● The GROW model was adopted as a template to conduct departmental and staff meetings.

● Middle Managers on the Leadership Development Programme spent time working in Action Learning Sets (see opposite). This involved devoting a discrete block of time on every occasion that the group met to allow small groups of approximately four people to help each other think through issues that were relevant and current for them, in a non-threatening, non-judgmental way.

 Each school has been able to transform some aspect of their school improvement in a way that suits their particular situation.

Dave Winter, Deputy Head, North Leamington Community School and Arts College

Group coaching

Many equate coaching with a one-to-one process. Yet, if coaching is essentially about reflecting on what is happening and deciding how we wish to move forward, there is no reason why it cannot be done collectively. Indeed, if we view coaching as less of a process and more of a philosophy then it is apparent that there are many variations around the theme.

Group coaching works best in groups of between three and six. The idea behind the groups is simple: each member in turn has an opportunity to raise an issue that is currently on his mind. The other members of the group help him think it through. They do this by listening, reflecting back, asking questions and so on – as opposed to judging, telling and 'solving' the issue for him.

People refer to these groups by different names, *Reflection Teams, Trust Groups* and *Action Learning Sets* being some of the more common currently in use. Some schools don't attach a label to these groups; they simply create time for groups of teachers to meet, talk and reflect. All are variations on a theme and are underpinned by the coaching philosophy of helping people help themselves.

Who does what?

All schools need to address a number of key questions:

1 Who coaches?

2 Who is coached?

3 Who coaches the coaches?

There is a compelling argument that the answers to the first two questions need to be *everyone* and *everyone*. For coaching – which involves individuals reflecting on, and making sense of, experience – is rooted in learning and we would surely want all teachers to be learners.

Yet in some schools some teachers (usually the good ones) coach, while other teachers (usually the weaker ones) are coached. The logic is obvious yet when we examine this model a little closer we appear to be placing some teachers in the role of learners while others remain as teachers. Are we suggesting therefore that some teachers need to be learners while others don't?

One possibility is to adopt an approach based upon *coaching triangles*, in which three teachers adopt the role of coach, coachee and coach-of-the-coach over a period of time. The diagram on page 60 explains this arrangement in more detail.

Coaching triangles

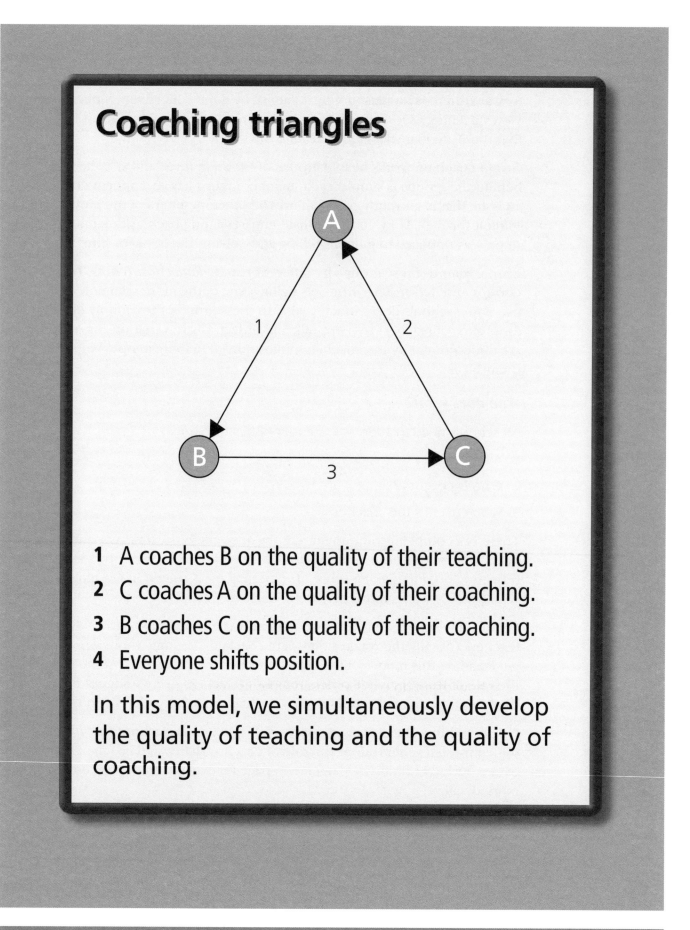

1 A coaches B on the quality of their teaching.
2 C coaches A on the quality of their coaching.
3 B coaches C on the quality of their coaching.
4 Everyone shifts position.

In this model, we simultaneously develop the quality of teaching and the quality of coaching.

Coaching the coaches

It is not coaching that has the potential to make an impact in schools – it is *high quality coaching*. So there are enormous implications concerning the coaching of the coaches.

Although a great many teachers have considerable experience of mentoring, few have extensive experience of coaching. Coaching requires a very different range of skills and techniques, and therefore, for many teachers, represents a significant shift in mindset. For although the difference between *I thought …* and *I noticed …* may seem slight (page 25), after many years of making judgements, having opinions and giving advice, the first instinct of many people is to *tell*. Moving into coaching mode involves, for many teachers, breaking the habit of a lifetime.

Consider the following:

- Many teachers receive an extremely limited amount of preparation – often just a day's training – before they begin coaching. Very few schools are investing in ongoing programmes to develop coaching expertise.

- Many people training teachers to coach have only limited experience of coaching themselves. As one teacher put it, *It was as if the trainer was reading the same book as we were - the only difference was that he was a page ahead.*

- Teachers are often trained to be coaches. Is there not a contradiction here? Do we need to train coaches or to coach them?

> **Reflect**
>
> In your school:
> - what kind of initial preparation do prospective coaches receive?
> - what provision do you make for the ongoing development of your coaches?
> - how often do your coaches observe other coaches at work?
> - how often do coaches observe themselves coach (on video)?

For further details of programmes focusing on 'coaching the coaches' offered by Mike Hughes *Education Training and Support*, see page 255.

Example: Methwold High School, Norfolk – *Coaching*

Denise Walker, Headteacher

Context

- 11–18 rural comprehensive
- NOR 800
- deemed to have 'serious weaknesses' in November 2003
- new Headteacher appointed September 2004

The Headteacher's story

When I took on the headship at Methwold High School, the brief was to improve the quality of learning and teaching across the curriculum. It would have been easy to adopt the approach of 'hitting colleagues over the head with a stick' to 'make them jump through hoops'! However, I judged that teachers already felt insecure following OFSTED and HMI visits and that they needed to be empowered, to share good practice and to support one another to improve their classroom practice.

Nine volunteers took up the offer to be coaches. These colleagues were prepared with help from Mike Hughes and soon led the way for others. They established coaching triads (see page 60), which enabled each to take the role of coachee, coach and coach-of-the-coach on a rolling programme. Immediately, the project fired cross-curricular debate about learning strategies and engaged colleagues who had lost confidence.

By the second year, these nine colleagues recruited others to the programme through their own enthusiasm and coached the new members to be coaches themselves. A culture of professional reflection, trust and dialogue was being established and teachers were talking about learning! Coaches were developing their personal expertise and we started to offer CPD to other schools. It was a great morale booster for teachers from a school with 'serious weaknesses' to be able to train teachers in other schools.

As we now approach the start of year three of the programme, the existing triads have divided again and from September 2006 *all* teachers (and several teaching assistants) will be involved. The culture of coaching has grown throughout the school and taken on a life of its own, without me, as the Headteacher, imposing it on everyone from the start. Colleagues are committed to the philosophy because they have ownership of the programme.

There has undoubtedly been a widespread and significant improvement in the quality of learning and teaching at Methwold and I am convinced that this has been due to the enthusiasm and confidence that we have gained from all being learners and from our coaching experiences.

The school came out of special measures in June 2006.

Example: Castle Vale School and Performing Arts College, Birmingham

Pete Weir, Assistant Headteacher

Context

● 11–16 secondary school

● NOR 885

● specialist Performing Arts College

Castle Vale School and Performing Arts College wanted to give colleagues the opportunity to develop fresh approaches to teaching and learning through an early finish every other Wednesday. As the Head expressed it at the launch, *This is an opportunity to do things differently, rather than more time to do things as they are.*

The sessions follow a basic pattern of four types of activity:

1 Departments work together on developing resources.

2 Coaching triads (see page 60) – cross-curricular groups, which run themselves, and complete an e-log of their ideas and activities. These have included peer observations, shared planning, lesson videoing, and lesson 'swaps' (colleagues planning lessons in a subject area of one of their triad members). These activities have been so highly valued that we have decided to pair triads up to ensure that there is a wider range of expertise in the groups. Each group will have one colleague who has had further coaching preparation.

3 Colleagues select one of the National Strategy's *Pedagogy and Practice* folders, and meet to discuss the materials and how they have used them. Teachers are asked to submit examples of new ideas they have used, which form an ever-growing appendix of the Teaching and Learning Policy.

4 Whole-staff sessions: colleagues present ideas for classroom practice.

This process has created an environment where discussion now focuses on creativity in our teaching and learning – in particular, developing strategies for:

● actively engaging all pupils in their learning

● ensuring that all pupils are challenged

● ensuring the development of thinking and group-work skills.

> " *I definitely feel more confident as a result of these Wednesday afternoon sessions ... I loved having the freedom to just discuss the areas of teaching and learning that we wanted and found useful ... this has undoubtedly raised staff morale, which then gives you the confidence to be even more experimental in the classroom.* "

Kerry Cooney – Second In Science

Consider the following questions

In your school ...

- Is there a shared understanding of learning?

- If you asked each teacher to write down a definition of the word 'learning', would they all write the same thing?

- Are you totally confident that:
  - all teachers know what learning looks like?
  - all students know what learning looks like?
  - all parents know what learning looks like?

- Do you have a written definition of the word 'learning' in your teaching and learning policy?

- If not, what made you decide you didn't need one?

- Is the school aligned? In terms of learning, do all teachers:
  - pull in the same direction?
  - pull in similar directions?
  - pull in different directions?

- How would other members of the institution respond to these questions?

- What do you take away from this exercise?

Section 2: Defining learning

Unless we know exactly where we are heading, it is difficult both to plot our course and to measure our progress.

Consider the following.

- If learning is our core business, the way we define it must surely inform the way in which we teach.

- Yet, despite widespread agreement that learning is the core business of schools, there is no single, universally accepted definition of learning within the world of education.

- Many schools fail to define learning.

- Without a shared definition of the word at either national or school level, we leave the interpretation of what is meant by learning to the individual. The danger is, of course, that if individual teachers interpret the term differently, they end up pulling in different directions.

- Good schools are aligned – if learning is to be the main thing, it follows that schools need a shared understanding of what learning actually is in order to ensure that everyone is pulling in the same direction.

- Schools either consider issues consciously and collectively, or leave them to chance.

Reflect

- How do you respond to the points made above?

- What would you wish to add to the list?

- Consider the questions on the opposite page.

Section 2 is written in three parts:

1 What is learning?

2 Creating a definition

3 Considering the implications

Learning – some thoughts

Learning occurs through the brain making its own meaning, making sense of things.

Paul Ginnis

Learning ... that reflective activity which enables the learner to draw upon previous experience to understand and evaluate the present, so as to shape future action and formulate new knowledge.

John Abbott

Turning mere facts into personal meaning is the central element in learning.

Colin Rose

The basic goal of education is understanding.

Howard Gardner

Each of us can learn only by making sense of what happens to us through actively constructing a world for ourselves.

Barnes and Todd

Learning ... an active process of making meaning that includes questioning, understanding, reflecting and making connections between existing and new information.

Barbara MacGilchrist, Kate Myers and Jane Reed

Central to deep learning is the notion of reflection i.e. the process by which information and experience are internalised and knowledge is created.

John West-Burnham

What is posited as knowledge is in fact information; not until the individual has absorbed the information, adapted it to the schemata already in his or her mind and discarded that which does not fit, only then can the individual be said to have knowledge. Knowledge is created, not transmitted.

Christopher Bowring-Carr and John West-Burnham

Knowledge is constructed and teaching is a matter of creating an environment for this.

Chris Watkins et al

Learning is an active process of constructing knowledge and developing understanding.

DfES

1 What is learning?

Learning is undoubtedly a complex, messy and highly personal process. A great many factors affect learning at an individual level, including motivation, self-belief and preferred learning styles.

However, despite the complexity and personal preferences, learning is essentially a meaning-making process. We may lack a single definition of the word, but there is broad consensus about the key principles involved and central to these is that learning is fundamentally about making sense – personal sense – of information and experience. This process of 'making meaning' involves individuals making connections between their existing knowledge and understanding of the world and any new information that they may encounter. It is therefore an active process, done *by* people, not *to* them; a product of *doing* rather than *receiving*.

> **Key principles of learning**
>
> ● Learning involves making *personal sense* of information and experiences.
>
> ● We make sense by making *connections* between what we already know and new inputs.
>
> ● Learning is therefore an *active* process.
>
> ● Learning is essentially a *reflective* process.

Teachers – at least, most teachers – know this. However, there are at least three good reasons for generating a definition of the word 'learning' and making an explicit commitment to the principles outlined above:

1 There are still some teachers who equate teaching with *telling*.

2 There is a real danger that learning is lost in the pressure cooker world of formal education, sacrificed in an attempt to cover the curriculum and pursue examination success.

3 The process of generating a definition is a healthy and worthwhile professional development activity in its own right.

It would be a mistake to underestimate the second point, above. Although OFSTED and the DfES now make explicit that learning is the priority in the classroom, teachers and schools continue to operate in a suffocating climate of accountability under the watchful eye of an unsympathetic PANDA. Teachers know that examination success keeps the PANDA happy and if the PANDA is happy, so too are OFSTED.

The need to deliver a still overcrowded curriculum and ensure that sufficient students jump through the examination hoop can exert a subtle yet significant pressure upon schools and teachers, and their understandable and often subconscious response is to focus on *telling* and *testing*.

Understanding is the 'Holy Grail' of the classroom, to be pursued, nurtured and cherished, for without it there can be no genuine learning.

Mike Hughes, *Closing the Learning Gap*

Some teachers' tendency to focus on *telling* may be understandable, but it is also regrettable and unnecessary. Learning and examination success are not mutually exclusive, and there are a great many successful schools and teachers who do place learning centre-stage, and always have done. The key point, however, is that this is too important an issue to be left to chance. If we want a school based upon learning, we have to make an *explicit* commitment to it, and that begins by establishing *precisely* what learning is.

2 Creating a definition

Maybe the nature and complexity of learning defies definition. However, if a total, conclusive and definitive definition ultimately proves elusive, the search for one will almost certainly deepen our understanding of learning and the learning process.

It may be easier to say what learning is not – behaving well and completing the task, for example, do not necessarily mean that learning has taken place.

We do not need an elaborate, jargon-riddled definition of the word, simply one that provides an unambiguous reminder that learning is more than replication and recall; learning involves *understanding*. For example:

> *Learning occurs when the penny drops, the light comes on and the learner says, 'ah, I get it!'*

A commitment to understanding

Essentially, we are seeking to draw attention to the centrality of understanding in the learning process, and provide all teachers with a constant reminder that:

- the fact that something has been taught does not necessarily mean that it has been learned
- the aim of the lesson must be for students to understand new information rather than just receive it
- the emphasis must therefore switch from teachers transferring information to helping students make sense of it – the mantra *What have they understood? How do you know?* is the yardstick on which all lessons must be evaluated.

Again, most teachers know these things. However, it is easy to forget in the hurly-burly of the classroom – particularly on a wet, windy Friday afternoon. Unless we make a conscious commitment to developing understanding, we run the risk of the many and varied distractions of the classroom diverting our attention away from the core purpose of the lesson.

> **Suggestion**
> Substitute the word 'understanding' for 'learning' in all of your documentation. Thus the Teaching and Learning Policy becomes the Teaching and Understanding Policy.

Humans never really cognitively understand or learn something until they can create a personal metaphor or model.

Eric Jenson

There are two broad approaches to arriving at a definition of learning available to schools:

1 Somebody – Headteacher or senior member of staff – selects a definition and informs the staff. In effect, a definition of learning is imposed on teachers.

2 A definition of the word is collectively generated by the entire institution. (This, of course, could include the students.)

The second option carries a number of benefits:

● Ownership – the fact that we've all heard the word before does not diminish its significance.

● The process of generating a definition is a worthwhile activity in its own right, as teachers will be forced to reflect and debate on their own understanding of the word; the more we understand learning, the more effectively we are able to teach.

● We end up with a definition suited for our school and our unique context.

Variations on a theme

John Abbot, the President of the 21st Century Learning initiative, refers to learning as, *the most gloriously messy, unstructured, mysterious process known to man.* It is indeed, as all teachers would surely testify, a complex process.

Classrooms are frenetic and emotionally charged environments and teachers, whose job it is to guide young, immature learners through the complexity of the learning process, are forced to operate at an instinctive, almost sub-conscious level. It is one of the reasons why so many well-meaning teaching and learning policies fail to impact on classroom practice; there just isn't time to thumb through the pages of a policy document – literally or mentally – before acting.

Consequently, *rules of thumb* can be very helpful in the context of the classroom. So too can visual images and metaphors for learning.

Creating a metaphor

Creating a metaphor, particularly when done collaboratively, is a powerful learning activity that requires reflection, thought and discussion. It is a process that helps deepen and develop understanding, while the product is an indication of the extent to which an issue has been grasped. As such, the strategy can be highly effective in the classroom. However, if we are committed to a school in which teachers are learners and buy into the principle that the more we understand about learning the better able we are to facilitate it in others, creating a metaphor for learning can prove to be an effective and worthwhile professional development activity for staff.

A metaphor for learning

The fruit machine metaphor

Learning occurs when the penny drops and the learner exclaims, 'ah, I get it!'

It may lack something in terms of scientific rigour, but this is a description of learning that a great many teachers instinctively recognise. It is also a straight-forward reminder that, despite the pressures, the object of the exercise is not to cover a syllabus (put pennies into the fruit machine) but to help students understand it (get pennies to drop).

Consider what happens when you play a fruit machine in an amusement arcade. The objective is to get the penny to drop; to get the penny to drop, you have to put a penny in. There are some parallels here with learning: the aim is the same – to get the penny to drop – and to get a penny to drop, there has to be a catalyst. In the context of the classroom, this catalyst is often, but by no means exclusively, the teacher. In other words, teachers often put the penny in.

Try this

Using the fruit machine as a metaphor for learning, continue the 'story' of the penny from the time it enters the machine to the time it finally drops. (The exercise works best when it is left as open-ended as possible.)

If you reject the metaphor, you have to:

- fully explain the reasons for your rejection
- offer an alternative metaphor for learning.

Points to consider:

- The object of the exercise is to get the penny to drop.

- The machine has to be switched on before anything is possible.

- Teachers have to 'play' 30 or so slightly different machines simultaneously.

- To get the penny to drop, someone has to put a penny in.

- You must use the correct currency – it is a waste of money putting coins in that the machine does not respond to (VAK?).

- There is no label telling you which currency to use – you must work it out.

- You can't see what is happening inside the machine, but presumably it is important (the unseen bit of learning is important – some learners think in a logical, sequential fashion while others naturally process information in a random, tangential manner).

- The penny doesn't drop until the lever is pulled (the role of the teacher is to prompt, guide, challenge and support the learner).

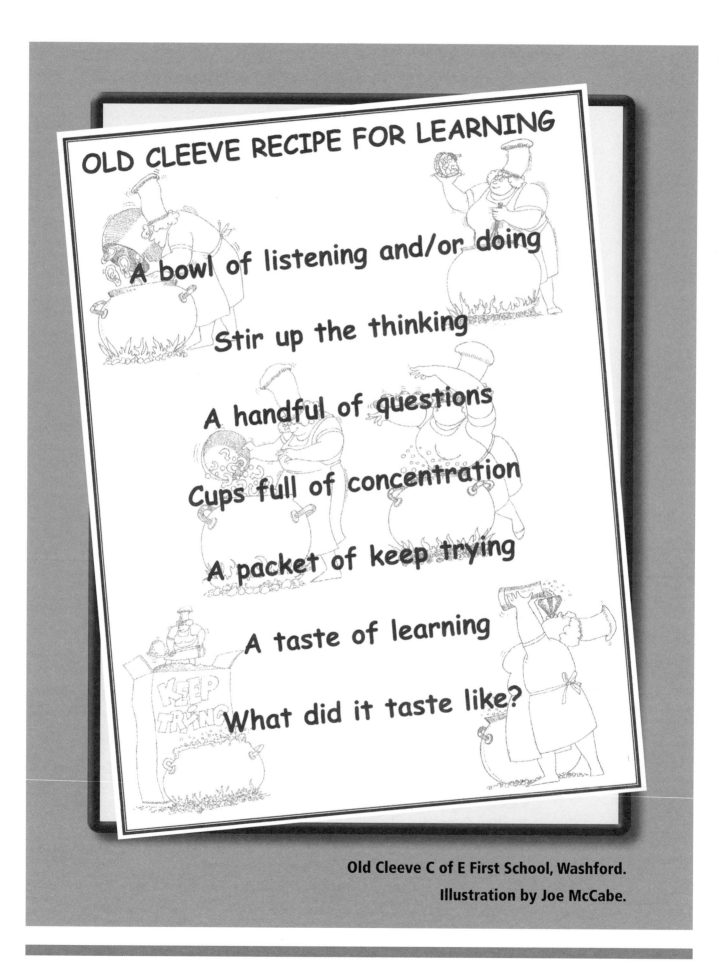

OLD CLEEVE RECIPE FOR LEARNING

A bowl of listening and/or doing

Stir up the thinking

A handful of questions

Cups full of concentration

A packet of keep trying

A taste of learning

What did it taste like?

Old Cleeve C of E First School, Washford.

Illustration by Joe McCabe.

- The penny will only drop when certain conditions are met – a line of cherries. Two cherries are insufficient – we require all three to hit the jackpot. Substantial learning will only occur when students:

  1 want to learn

  2 believe they can succeed

  3 are engaged in an active, meaningful process.

  Thus, the three cherries might be motivation, self-belief and engagement.

- You might not get all three cherries every lesson – but you can use the hold button.

- We don't *control* the three cherries (we cannot *make* students understand or *give* them self-belief and motivation) – but we do *influence* them and can create the conditions where these three crucial factors will be more likely. In other words you get a nudge!

- Sometimes lots of pennies drop at once. Some may roll away and be lost. It is important to be aware when the penny has dropped and to put the coins somewhere safe for future use.

- Teachers set the payout level. Students will become bored if the penny always drops and things are too easy but they will become dispirited if the penny only drops occasionally. Getting the payout level, or the degree of challenge, right is a key task for the teacher.

- We have a choice when the penny drops – tell students to keep it safely until they are required to get all their pennies out (examination day!) or re-invest it and see if we can help students deepen their understanding still further.

The fruit machine metaphor means something to the teachers who created it – it is their metaphor. Not only does it mean something, it influences practice as the image – which is laminated to all teachers' desks – is a constant reminder that:

- the aim of the exercise is to get pennies to drop – understanding

- putting the penny in does not guarantee it will drop – telling students and transferring information does not guarantee they will understand it

- there is always hope – it doesn't matter how many times you have put the penny in without success, the next one could hit the jackpot!

Which best describes your classroom?

The focus is on learning.	The focus is on teaching.
I teach in the way students learn.	Students are expected to learn in the way I teach.
I strive to create an atmosphere conducive to learning.	I strive to create an atmosphere conducive to teaching.
We talk about learning.	We talk about work.
Students are actively encouraged to talk about their learning.	Students are often required to work in silence.
Students learn collaboratively.	Students usually learn alone.
Students ask questions.	Students answer questions.
I seek commitment.	I seek compliance.
I focus on motivation.	I focus on behaviour.

3 Considering the implications

Defining learning is only the starting point; the real issue is what we do about it. For if learning is indeed to be the main thing, everything from policies to pedagogy must be informed by it. Teaching in particular must be a response to how we define learning. In simple terms, teachers must teach in the way children learn, rather than expect children to learn in the way they teach.

> **Reflect**
>
> Which of the following statements most accurately reflects your classrooms?
>
> ● Teachers teach in the way children learn.
>
> ● Children are expected to learn in the way teachers teach.

A more detailed consideration of this whole issue forms the basis of *Closing the Learning Gap* by Mike Hughes – details on page 253.

The procedure outlined below is a suggested approach designed to ensure that the school places learning centre-stage, and is based upon the needs of learners.

Step one

In order to establish a clear picture of what you believe learning to be and the conditions required for effective learning to take place, respond to the following prompt:

Children learn effectively when they ...

Possible responses might include statements such as:

● *have frequent opportunities to learn in their preferred style*

● *are challenged at an appropriate level*

● *feel safe and valued*

And so on.

Step two

Consider appropriate responses to the list generated in step one by addressing the following. (This can be done at whole-school, department or individual level.)

So therefore we must ...

● *provide a variety of learning experiences in the classroom to accommodate different learners*

● *ensure that children are working in their personal zone of challenge* (see page 40)

And so on.

Extract from the Teaching and Learning Policy of Ecclesall Junior School, Sheffield

We believe children learn best when:

1   they are happy
2   they are treated with respect
3   all aspects of their development are seen to be of equal worth
4   they work in a stimulating environment
5   the school is well ordered
6   they are given a broad range of learning experiences
7   they are set tasks that are appropriately demanding
8   they are given the freedom to organise some of their own learning
9   they have the opportunity to develop and discover a range of new interests

To help children be happy we will:

1.1   greet them with a smile

1.2   make them feel safe, both physically and emotionally

1.3   listen to them when things go wrong

1.4   criticise poor behaviour, not the child

1.5   be firm but forgiving

1.6   be fair and consistent in our own behaviour

In treating children with respect we will:

2.1   use their names correctly

2.2   praise each child more than we grumble

2.3   value each child's contribution

2.4   take every opportunity to give positive feedback to everyone

2.5   recognise that children learn in different ways and teach accordingly

2.6   set a personal example that is consistent with what we expect from the children

2.7   show interest when they talk to us

2.8   maintain high expectations

And so on.

The key to this step is to be *explicit* and leave as little as possible up to individual interpretation. For example, few teachers would disagree with the need to create a supportive learning environment in which children feel safe and valued. But what does this mean in concrete terms? It means, of course that teachers use children's first names, smile at them, praise more than rebuke, take an interest in their life outside of school and so on.

Similarly, few would argue that teachers should provide a variety of learning experiences. However, what does this mean in practice? One possible approach is to create a *minimum entitlement* for all children. For example, we make an explicit commitment that all children will be able to work in their preferred style at least once during each unit of work, or each week, or each a day.

Step three

Convert the statements and commitments generated in step two into concrete strategies that teachers can use in the classroom, and build them into schemes of work.

This is the key, yet often neglected, step. For simply agreeing that children learn best when they are able to learn in their preferred style and accepting that the onus is on the teacher and school to provide a variety of learning experiences will remain empty rhetoric unless individual teachers are crystal clear about how the intentions articulated during steps one and two translate into practice.

The challenge is to turn aspirations into activities. One possible approach is to work collectively to generate a bank of resources or handbook of good ideas that teachers can dip into. For example, generate a handbook of good ideas for kinaesthetic learners or a booklet giving '101 ways to generate curiosity' (see page 211) and so on.

Step four

Compare the reality with the goal. (See the GROW model on page 37.)

Steps one and two establish our goal. This is the situation in the classroom that we are aiming for. We must now hold ourselves to account and consider the extent to which our current practice (reality) matches up to our stated intentions.

For example, we said that we would smile at children – are we? We said that children learn best when they are challenged at an appropriate level and therefore we would endeavour to keep children in the *zone of challenge* as much as possible – how successful are we at this? (Use the zone of challenge graph on page 40 to address this particular issue.)

One final thought: many schools have a teaching and learning policy that broadly addresses steps one and two. However, very few schools see this through and complete steps three and four.

A focus on learning demands that we first establish what effective learning looks like before considering the implications for teaching and structuring lessons.

In this way, pedagogy is derived from a desire to facilitate learning rather than produce good teaching.

Section 3: A lesson template based explicitly on learning

If we want something to happen, we have to say so. While making such a statement does not guarantee that it will happen, making something explicit does make it more likely.

Having defined learning, we must now ensure that lessons are based upon it. One of the most effective ways of doing this is to adopt a common lesson structure *explicitly* based upon learning.

Critics of a common lesson structure highlight the fact that learning is a complex process and does not fit neatly into a rigid and potentially restrictive framework. They argue that a standard lesson template can actually limit learning by curtailing spontaneity and creativity.

Certainly learning is a complex, messy and individual business that cannot be neatly boxed or placed in a straightjacket. However, a common lesson template need not be rigid or restrictive and – provided it is viewed as a loose, flexible framework on which to base teaching and learning – it can be enormously beneficial. Not only does it promote internal consistency, it provides a clear, unambiguous structure for planning, reflection, training and teaching.

We are therefore seeking a framework that ...
- promotes internal consistency and aligns the institution
- keeps the focus explicitly on learning.

... while recognising that ...
- learning is messy, individual and unpredictable
- there is no one way to learn – therefore, there can be no one way to teach
- there are exceptions to every rule
- great teaching and learning involve spontaneity, creativity and flexibility.

Choosing a structure

For many schools, the question is not so much whether to adopt a common lesson structure, but which particular template to adopt. Three issues are crucial here:

> 1 Is the template based upon teaching or learning?
> 2 Is the template manageable?
> 3 Is the template flexible?

Things should be made as simple as possible, but not more so.

Albert Einstein

1 Does the structure focus on teaching or learning?

One of the key potential benefits of adopting a common lesson structure is that it has the potential to align the institution by *explicitly* focusing upon learning. Yet many lesson structures are based not upon learning but around teaching. Three- or four-part lessons based broadly around a starter, middle and plenary are essentially a way to organise teaching. This does not mean that students don't learn in these lessons; rather that the focus of the template is teaching, and learning is implicit rather than centre-stage.

To an extent, such structures have been successful in recent years as part of a concerted effort to improve *teaching*. However, the focus of attention has clearly shifted and the challenge for many schools is how to switch the emphasis from teaching to *learning*; from a largely transfer-of-information approach to one that fully engages learners in an active process.

If it is accepted that learning essentially involves *receiving information* and *making sense* of it, there is a strong argument that this difference should be made explicit by our lesson structure. If learning is our aim, learning must be our focus.

2 Is the structure manageable?

As a broad rule of thumb, the more discrete phases in the template, the more difficult it is for teachers to hold the model in their heads. There is no need to over complicate a process that is already complicated enough in its own right. For amid the undoubted complexity, learning essentially consists of two discrete yet related phases: receiving information, and making sense of it. Let us remember that the purpose of a model is to *simplify* reality.

3 Is the structure flexible?

Learning is not always a sequential process – nor, therefore, a cyclical one. C does not always follow B, which does not always follow A. Our model – which should be as 'simple as possible but not more so' (opposite) – must be flexible enough to take this factor into account.

Reflect

- Do you currently adopt a common lesson template?
- What was the thinking behind your decision?
- If you do use one, is your template based upon teaching or learning?
- Does the template explicitly refer to aspects of the learning process?

It is not sufficient to be engaged in activity; without reflection, the learning potential is lost.

Chris Watkins et al
Institute of Education, University of London
NSIN Research Matters Summer 2002

A suggested approach

The following model has been used in classrooms, both Primary and Secondary, since the beginning of the nineties. It is sometimes referred to as the four-phase lesson, which is a little misleading as it is actually based upon four phases or aspects of the learning process. It first appeared in print in *Strategies for Closing the Learning Gap* (2001), by Mike Hughes – details on page 253.

> It is a model that is based upon three key principles reflecting the way in which people learn:
>
> **1** making sense
> **2** context and connections
> **3** reflection.

1 Making sense

Learning involves making sense of information. This is not the same as receiving information, and it is suggested that this distinction must:

- lie at the heart of any lesson structure based upon learning
- be made explicit.

In reality, the boundary between receiving new information and making sense of it is incredibly blurred. However, by making the distinction between the two, we are highlighting, and providing a constant reminder, that receiving information does not equate to understanding; the fact that it has been taught does not mean that it has been learned.

2 Context and connections

Deep, meaningful learning involves understanding. Understanding involves connecting and incorporating new information into our existing understanding of the world. Teachers can help students make these connections by explicitly connecting the learning – often, but not exclusively, at the beginning of the lesson – and helping students place the new information and specific detail of a lesson into a wider context.

3 Reflection

In recent years, there has been an increasing acceptance of the fact that learning involves *doing*, and is more than passively receiving information. Consequently, we see far greater student activity in classrooms, and learning has arguably improved as a result.

However, as Watkins et al argue opposite, *doing* alone is insufficient to promote meaningful learning. At the risk of gross oversimplification, it can be argued that *reflection* is the aspect of the learning process most neglected in classrooms.

Dissecting a lesson

Use this exercise to prompt reflection and generate discussion, thereby deepening understanding of learning. It works best when two or more teachers work independently and then compare notes.

Learning consists of four discrete yet inextricably linked elements:

NI **new information** or experience

CC making **connections** and placing new information in a wider **context**

MS **making sense** of new information or experience

RR **reflecting** on and **reviewing** learning.

Procedure

1 Observe a video-recorded lesson. Pause after 15 minutes and consider the balance between the four elements of learning above.

2 Allocate 12 marks to reflect the emphasis. For example, a lesson segment that was completely focussed on transferring new information might score **NI** 12, **CC** 0, **MS** 0 and **RR** 0. A later segment might show a different balance, such as **NI** 4, **CC** 6, **MS** 2, **RR** 0. Repeat the process after another 15 minutes, and again 15 minutes later, and so on. All 12 marks must be allocated, for each 15-minute segment.

3 Note that your mark allocation should reflect the relative emphasis on each element of learning, not simply the proportion of time dedicated to it. For example, there may be a strong element of reflection during a lesson segment, even though a relatively small amount of time was devoted to it.

4 Record you mark allocations on simple axes. For example:

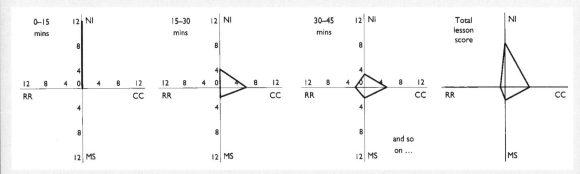

5 Carry out this exercise over a series of lessons. What do your graphs tell you about the learning that is taking place in your classroom?

A learning framework

The aspects of the learning process outlined on page 85 may be translated into a basic learning framework as shown below.

1 Context
- Provide a context for learning
- Connect the lesson to prior learning
- Share explicit learning objectives
- Provide an overview of the lesson
- Stimulate curiosity and provide a sense of challenge

2 New information
- Instruction, demonstration, exposition, and/or a problem to be solved

3 Making sense
- Processing
- Developing, demonstrating and assessing understanding
- Doing

4 Reflect and Review
- What has been learned?
- How it has been learned?

It is important to point out that:

- the model is a broad and flexible framework, not a rigid template
- the model refers to a learning experience, not a lesson as such – the experience may last for ten minutes, or for three weeks
- precise interpretation of the model will vary enormously in different subjects and different situations
- boundaries between the phases will almost certainly be blurred
- the phases are not necessarily sequential
- teachers may well scroll through these phases several times during a lesson
- there are no guarantees – teachers cannot *make* students understand
- while the structure of the experience is significant, it will be the quality of the tasks and the interaction that will largely determine the quality of learning
- interpretation is the key – great learning always has and always will involve spontaneity, creativity and flexibility.

The City Academy BRISTOL

CITY ACADEMIES   SPORTS COLLEGES

	TEACHER OBSERVABLE INDICATORS	EVIDENCE
PHASE 1	**Create a relaxed, purposeful atmosphere** – greet students at the door/smile/use first names **Link session to prior learning** – Think of the three most important things that you learned last lesson/In two minutes I am going to ask you what you learned last lesson Begin session in an interesting/novel/unexpected way – **engages students** Asking **open questions** Pose a problem to be solved. Get students to generate questions. Set a **challenge**. Set targets **Ensure students know what to look for** during the session **Share learning objectives** with students – By the end of today's session you will all know/understand/be able to … Provide an **overview**	
PHASE 2 Receiving information	Present information in **short chunks** Ask a **variety of closed and open questions** New information is delivered in a **variety of ways to suit different learning preferences** – VAKT Exposition, Audio visual aids – video clips, etc, Text books, Graphs, diagrams, pictures and so on, ICT – CD-ROM/Internet, Demonstrations Use of appropriate technical language Check students' understanding **Inputs are punctuated with tasks and activities designed to develop understanding**	
PHASE 3 Making sense	HELPING STUDENTS LEARN *Quality* of tasks and interactions that is important Ask a large proportion of **open questions**. Allow processing time for students to think before further intervention Allow students to **talk to each other** Ask **supplementary or extension questions** to **extend understanding** Ask questions to encourage students to **reflect upon their thinking** Encouraging/reassuring, Guiding, Prompting, Challenging thinking Help students to **reframe experiences by prompting, paraphrasing and reflecting** Frequency of opportunities for students to generate questions Encourage pair- or group-generated questions Teacher encourages group to think what question they might ask Assess understanding Ask students to **REDUCE** information. Ask students to **TRANSFORM** information **Listen** to students explaining something	
PHASE 4 Review	Teacher asks the students **what they have learned** – what are the 3 most interesting things you've learned today? What questions could you answer now that you couldn't answer at the beginning of the session? Provide guidance to students **Open-ended questioning** Prime brains about **what they will be learning next lesson** – presented as a question/problem or riddle Smile! Sending a clear message that I enjoyed that learning session and am looking forward to working with the group next session.	

'Plenary' or 'reflection'?

> **Reflect**
>
> ● Which is generally done better in your school, the beginning of lessons or the end?
>
> ● Which is the stronger feature of lessons in your school, students engaged in activity or students reflecting on their learning at a metacognitive level?

Consider the following:

● In the vast majority of schools, lessons begin more effectively than they end.

● Students are increasingly active during lessons. However, while active engagement in learning is essential, so to is reflecting upon the experience, and it is reflecting upon learning that is often neglected in the classroom.

● If this is accepted, then it may provide the focus for the next step of our never-ending efforts to improve learning in the classroom.

Many people talk these days about the need to 'do' a plenary. However, *doing* a plenary does not necessarily enhance learning; consciously reflecting on the learning experience does.

According to the dictionary, the word plenary means *'full or complete'* and in the context of the classroom it is usually associated with coming together. It is therefore essentially a way to organise *teaching*. Crucially, the word provides no clue as to what students should be doing when they have come together. Reflection, on the other hand, is an integral part of the *learning* process, and **if we want something to happen then we have to say so** – explicitly.

Consider the following:

1 Lesson templates that end with a plenary imply that reflection (assuming that the plenary involves students reflecting) is something done at the end of the lesson. Ideally, reflecting upon learning is something that pervades the entire experience.

2 Although fewer lessons end in time-honoured *oh no, is that the time* fashion, many plenaries are little more than a summary of the lesson. At their worst, they involve teachers summarising what students *should have* learned – as opposed to students reflecting on what *has been* learned.

3 Many lessons end up with a plenary designed to *review* information rather than *reflect* upon learning. In crude terms, reviewing information is essentially about memory and recall, while reflecting upon information and experience is essentially about understanding. Both are important in the context of school learning. The problem comes when information is reviewed at the expense of reflection.

4 Learning is enhanced when students become better learners and this demands that we reflect upon not only *what* was learned but also *how* it was learned.

		STUDENTS OBSERVABLE INDICATORS	EVIDENCE
PHASE 1		Students immediately **settle down to work** Students **explain something** to the teacher/partner/group Students generate questions/own targets Reduce information Transform information	
PHASE 2	**Receiving information**	Listen to information Watch visual stimulus **Read information** **Doing ...**	
PHASE 3	**Making sense**	Sharing ideas Experimenting Exploring ideas Judging their own and others' performance Answering in depth – Using analysis and evaluation Teaching each other Students **explain something** to the teacher/partner/group Students carry out a piece of **research and report back** to the rest of the class/group etc Peer coaching **Recreate** rather than reproduce information **Demonstrate** understanding **Reduce** information – Summarise in 100 words/Rank order the following statements/Which is the most important statement?/What is the most important section of the diagram? **Changing** information – convert this text into a diagram, picture, cartoon strip/Describe in your own words/Use the key words in a poem/piece of music	
PHASE 4	**Review**	**Students themselves identify what they have learned** **Demonstrate** knowledge of what they have learned – **explanation** Students **reflecting on what they have learned**/How they tackled a particular task/What they would do differently next time	

It is important to emphasise that there is no suggestion here that reflection cannot take place in a plenary. Nor is it suggested that a lesson template that includes the word 'plenary' precludes reflecting upon learning throughout the duration of the lesson. The issue, however, is that while a great many teachers regularly conclude lessons with a meaningful, reflective plenary *and* weave reflection through their lessons as a continuous thread, not all do.

'Lesson plan' or 'learning plan'?

Classroom – a place where 30 students go to watch a teacher working.

Teachers have traditionally planned lessons. We even have pro-formas known as lesson plans. In some schools, there is a requirement for teachers to complete these forms and submit them to be monitored. Not surprisingly, teachers consider in advance how they are going to *teach* a lesson – which resources they are going to use, how they are going to transfer information, how they are going to structure the lesson, and so on.

Much less attention has generally been given to how students are going to learn.

Consider the following:

> Peeping into the classroom we notice that the students are gathered around the front desk. On it sits a kettle. Amid the inevitable cup-of-tea jokes, the teacher flicks the switch and begins. Although we can't hear every word, we can hear sufficiently well to get the gist: … *source of heat … evaporates surface moisture … vapour …*
>
> Every so often, the teacher breaks away to write up key words on the whiteboard - EVAPORATION, CONVECTION, VAPOUR – before returning to the kettle: … *What do you notice about the steam? Yes, it's rising … just like the warm air … Watch what happens next,* urges the teacher and holds his hand in the path of the steam (at a safe distance!). Tiny droplets of water begin to form on his palm …

At first glance, it appears an interesting enough lesson – certainly, it is a bit different and the teacher would appear to be doing a good job. However, when we consider things from the perspective of the students we get a slightly different picture, for, despite the obvious novelty of the situation, the students are simply being required to watch and listen.

This is not to criticise the use of the kettle or decry the explanation provided by the teacher. The vignette above is clearly just a snapshot, not the whole lesson and such a demonstration can play a valuable role in helping students learn. Much, of course, depends on what the students were required to do with their new information during the remainder of the period.

The Cavendish School & Sports College
Lesson Plan

| Date |
| Period |

| | | Class: | | Room: | |

| Teacher: | | | | | |
| Number of students: | Total – Boys – Girls - | Level of ability of group: | | | |

Special Needs/Learning Information: *include information about targets for students with IEPs and Statements*

Context of lesson

Learning Aims/Outcomes:
All –
Most –
A few -

Connect learning:

| Receiving information | Understanding/making sense |

Review and Reflect

Other information (e.g. risk assessment, Health and safety)

Homework:

Please attach class list, seating plan & prior attainment data for group to this sheet and hand it to the observer as soon as they come to the lesson

The purpose of recounting this incident is to draw attention to the fact that we sometimes get a different perspective on a lesson when we look through the eyes of a student. Two key questions that should be at the forefront of our minds when either planning or observing a lesson are:

1   What are the students required to *do*?

2   How is this helping them *learn*?

> **Reflect**
>
> Do you plan how you are going to teach a lesson, or how students are going to learn?

These are two very simple strategies to keep the focus upon learning:

1 **Split all lesson plan and lesson observation pro-formas into two.** This forces teachers to reflect upon and consciously plan for what students will be doing. In short, we plan learning as well as teaching.

An example of the lesson planning sheet used at Cavendish School, Hemel Hempstead, can be found opposite.

2 **Plan learning experiences, not lessons.** Learning experiences can last three minutes or three weeks – and there may well be more than one in each lesson. In any meaningful learning experience, you will almost certainly find:

● a catalyst – some new information and/or experience

● an element of connecting and contextualising that information or experience

● learners making meaning

● an element of reflection.

> **Suggestion**
>
> When writing notes during a lesson observation, begin all sentences with the phrase '*The students were ...*' Continue with '*... because ...*'
>
> This simple approach ensures that the focus of the observation is on learners and learning.
>
> Thanks to David Potter for this highly effective strategy.

saltash.net community school
Four-Phase Learning Experience

Evidence

Overview
- Teacher creates a relaxed yet purposeful atmosphere

- Lesson is linked to students' prior knowledge
- Lesson is placed in a wider context – students are provided with an overview

- Specific learning objectives are shared with the students?
- Do the students know what to look for during the lesson?

- Is there a sense of curiosity, challenge and expectation?
- How quickly is the key learning point introduced?

Input
- Is information delivered in easily digestible chunks?

- To what extent was the input multisensory – Multiple Intelligences, Visual, Auditory, Kinaesthetic?

- As a rough guide the average concentration span of the students is about age + 2 mins

Process
- Frequent teacher-student and student-student interaction
- An emphasis on students re-creating rather than reproducing information
- Strategies were employed to develop understanding
- Students given the opportunity to demonstrate understanding
- Teacher was able to assess how much had been understood

- Tick if any of the following strategies were used.
1. verbalising
2. reduction
3. transformation
4. teaching something
5. sequencing
6. 'It's like..'
7. predicting
8. classifying
9. problem solving/investigations/enquiry
10. creating learning maps
11. rank ordering
12. higher-order questioning
13. thinking about thinking
14. understanding the question
15. students asking questions

- What was the ratio of time students spent receiving information to the time spent making sense of it?

Reflect and Review
- Was the review linked to the learning objectives?

- Were students actively involved in the review process?

- Students encouraged to reflect on *how* they have learned

This is one page of a double-page spread. The facing page contains current OFSTED criteria.

Example: saltash.net community school – *adopting the 'four-phase' learning template*

Karl Sampson, Deputy Headteacher, saltash.net community school

Context

- 11–18 mixed comprehensive school in south-east Cornwall
- NOR 1354
- combined specialism in Science, Mathematics and Computing with a Rural Dimension

The appointment of a Deputy Headteacher with responsibility for developing the quality of learning was one of a series of changes introduced as a result of the direction being taken by a newly appointed Headteacher. The brief for this new appointment was simple and straightforward: to place learning – and, more importantly, collaborative learning – at the heart of school improvement.

This coincided beautifully with the designation of specialist status and its emphasis on whole-school improvement. One of the first things that we did was to take our mantra from Stephen Covey – *The main thing, is to keep the main thing, the main thing* – and for us the main thing is learning.

Why adopt a learning experience template?

An examination of the school's existing lesson observation sheet (based on the old OFSTED model) highlighted the lack of explicit reference to learning. Indeed, learning was relegated to the last line of the sheet. If staff were not being engaged in a discussion about learning as part of lesson observation and feedback, then when was this dialogue taking place?

We were aware that:

> *Talk in classrooms is mainly about work, sometimes about performance, and rarely about learning. At best 2% of classroom interactions are about learning and how it may be advanced.*
>
> Chris Watkins et al, NSIN Research Matters 2002

We felt that the adoption of a learning experience template would act as the catalyst for a regular dialogue about learning to take place both in and outside of the classroom.

Why this particular template?

I had used this particular template very successfully over the last four years at Tring School in Hertfordshire. I knew, therefore, that it was tried and tested, but more importantly it had credibility amongst colleagues and reflected their experiences in the classroom. I cannot emphasise the importance of this particular point enough. The beauty of this template is that it reflects the way that we learn, and follows the KISS principle – Keep It Simple Silly! To share learning objectives, provide new information, give students tasks and time to process and make sense of this, and then review and reflect on what has been learned is not new to most teachers. However, this was now being made *explicit,* with learning rather than content coverage becoming the key focus for the structured professional dialogue which was taking place.

We live in a knowledge-rich society whose knowledge base doubles every 373 days, and therefore teaching knowledge is fast becoming an anachronism. As a group of teachers, we felt that it was much more appropriate to chase the learning dispositions and equip people to be able to deal with, make sense of and use this knowledge. The 'four-phase' lesson template provided us with a vehicle to do this most effectively.

Introducing the template

An Inset day in September 2004 was used as an opportunity for staff to establish a collective definition of learning, its characteristics, what it looks like, feels like and when it is most effective. It was the first opportunity that they had ever had as a group to discuss, debate and shape their individual views about learning into collective values.

The 'four-phase' learning experience was then introduced to the newly formed Learning Group. The meeting was voluntary and involved over 20 staff reflecting upon and discussing their own practice. We did this by spending the first 25 minutes looking at Mike Hughes' *Four-Phase Template for Learning.* We were able to look at the model as a whole and then reflect upon each phase as it applied to our own teaching through a series of question prompts and discussion. This was then followed by a whole-group discussion about the merits of the activity and its implications for our practice. There was a terrific buzz around the room and it was great to see and hear colleagues so engaged and animated about their classroom practice.

We then moved on to how we might use the *Four-Phase Template for Learning* to develop a system of peer observation that focuses far more heavily on learning than the current lesson observation sheet. By making this move, it was felt that we would be better able to discuss and analyse learning as well as examine how the conditions for it to take place most effectively are created.

Finally, we paired up with another teacher and agreed that by our next meeting we would have planned, taught and observed a lesson using the *Four-Phase Template for Learning,* thereby allowing us to test its validity in the classroom. At the start of the next meeting, we each shared a piece of effective practice we had observed, thus giving us the perfect platform on which to engage in a professional dialogue about what constitutes effective learning, the impact of the lesson template and the implications for teaching.

How is it used in practice?

Feedback was unanimously and overwhelmingly positive, with many staff telling departmental colleagues about it. Soon there was a clamour for it to be introduced more widely across the school. However, we had to bear in mind the changing national agenda and the new OFSTED framework which emphasised self-evaluation. Since we were changing our lesson observation sheets, we decided to incorporate the two changes at the same time (see page 94).

This now forms the bedrock of our quality assurance procedures and allows us to keep the *Four-Phase Template* and its emphasis on learning at the heart of our work, whilst at the same time setting it alongside the criteria used by OFSTED, highlighting the fact that the two are not mutually exclusive. Indeed, an OFSTED inspection in November 2005 acknowledged that:

... the new styles of lesson observation are improving the quality of teaching and learning for students. Good practice is being shared between teachers.

Outcomes

- This process has provided an opportunity for all staff to engage in an ongoing dialogue and debate about learning and teaching whilst developing a shared/common vocabulary.

- It has enabled all members of this school to translate their values into collective practice.

- It has provided a clarity of purpose and practice by articulating tacit knowledge, the implicit and intuitive.

- It sits at the heart of our self-evaluation and quality assurance processes and promotes consistency of experience – a characteristic feature of good and improving schools.

- It has established a minimum entitlement for all students and staff alike.

- It has provided teachers with a series of rules of thumb that they can confidently use and adapt for themselves, as well as share and develop with their colleagues.

Next steps

Over the next year, our aim is to produce a handbook of effective practice that reflects our new Learning and Teaching Policy and spotlights the good practice that is being identified. This handbook will have contributions from all departments, the idea being to tie theory and practice together through a collaborative venture built around sharing practice.

The idea is based around the theme of the Paul Ginnis book *The Teacher's Toolkit*. By the end of the next academic year, we will have our own Learning and Teaching Policy (the principles of what we do) built around the four-phase learning experience framework (the structure that supports what we do) and underpinned by our own handbook of practical ideas (the successful strategies that we use) as we collectively create our own saltash.net community school Teacher's Toolkit.

 The adoption of the four-phase lesson structure, as a common policy by our staff, has been one of the most significant steps we have taken at our school in order to ensure a consistently high quality of teaching and an improved learning experience for our students across all three key stages.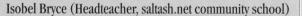

Isobel Bryce (Headteacher, saltash.net community school)

Between 2002 and 2005, the percentage of students at City Academy Bristol who gained five or more A*–C grades at GCSE rose from 33% to 52%.

In December 2005, OFSTED reported that:

- *in 2005, GCSE results rose impressively, shattering the challenging targets*

- *students are really proud of the Academy – they know their views are sought, valued and used*

- *students really enjoy reviewing practice and have very good ideas about what to do next.*

Example: City Academy Bristol

Becky Pearce, Assistant Headteacher

Context

- 11–18 City Academy

- NOR 1282

Background

September 2003: The Academy adopted what is often referred to as the 'four-phase' lesson (as outlined on page 87) as a template for lesson planning and teaching.

The rationale was simple: we wanted to base teaching and learning upon a standard template in order to establish a consistency of experience between classrooms. We adopted this particular template because it is both simple and flexible, and crucially focuses explicitly upon learning.

Whilst we stressed that the model should not been seen as restrictive, and that teachers should use it flexibly, we also established concrete *observable indicators* – elements of teaching and learning that we would normally expect to see in each of the four phases (see pages 88 and 90). These indicators in turn provided us with an unambiguous *minimum standard expectation* for lessons that was universally understood by teachers.

September 2005: the use of the template expanded and the four-phase lesson is now the structure on which we base:

- lesson planning

- staff development

- coaching

- student evaluation.

Focusing on specific aspects

We adopted a modular approach to staff development and improvement, with the academic year being split into five modules of approximately seven weeks:

1 lesson starts

2 transferring information

3 making sense

4 reflect and review

5 miscellaneous.

During each module, all staff development, coaching and student evaluation are focussed exclusively on the relevant element of the lesson. For example, during module one, the focus for all training and staff development workshops, all peer observations, all coaching and all student evaluations, is on lesson starts. Professional Reflection (Inset) Days are built into the programme and also focus upon the discrete phase in question. (Note: routine monitoring observations run alongside this programme.)

The City Academy
BRISTOL

CITY ACADEMIES

SPORTS COLLEGES

IMPROVING HOW YOUR LEARNING SESSIONS START ...
STUDENT VOICE SURVEY

Please tick the box that best fits what your teachers do.

TEACHERS:	TRUE OF NEARLY ALL TEACHESR	TRUE OF MOST TEACHERS	TRUE OF SOME TEACHERS	TRUE OF ONLY A FEW TEACHERS
Greet you individually at the start of each session				
Let us know what is expected of us				
Grab our attention right from the start				
Share with us what we are learning about in the session				
Make the beginnings of our sessions interesting				
Make us think and solve problems				
Link what we are to learn to prior sessions				
Go over what we should have learned in the last session				
Enable us to discuss things in groups				
Enable us to discuss things in pairs				
Enable us to discuss things as a class				
Encourage us to ask questions				

WHAT WOULD YOU LIKE TEACHERS TO DO IN THE STARTER THAT IS NOT ON THIS LIST?

Student voice

The **Student Aspiration Group** meets every Friday, comprising of two representatives from each Learning Family. (The school is divided into Learning Families – tutor groups – with between 12 and 16 students in each family.) Each week a different year group will meet (one week it will be representatives from Y7 Learning Families, the next week Y8, and so on). Different students represent the group on each occasion, so that by the end of the year every student has had their voice heard.

These sessions are used to reflect upon the experiences that students have in the classroom, discuss what makes a good lesson from a student's viewpoint, outline what students find helpful in terms of assessment procedures, and so on. During module one the focus for these sessions will be lesson starts, during module two, receiving information, and so on.

Students from Y8 and Y9 also ran a **student workshop** as part of a Professional Reflection Day, which proved popular and was well attended by staff. During their workshop they outlined what they felt makes a good learning session and what students find helpful in the classroom. This was based in part upon a survey that had been conducted by Y8 and Y9 students. The students later made a similar presentation to the Governors.

From September 2006, the intention is for students to participate in lesson observations and attend selected meetings on the calendar.

Professional pathways

During 2005/06, all staff participated in a coaching pilot programme based around coaching triangles (see page 60) and experienced coaching, being coached and coaching the coach. Although the programme was successful in many ways, it was noticeable that teachers had no choice in their personal development and no time in which to pursue it.

Therefore, from September 2006 all teachers will be able to choose which professional development pathway they wish to follow from a menu of:

- peer observation
- coaching
- lesson observation

with the five modules outlined on page 99 providing the focus for all observation and coaching during the relevant period. (The main difference between peer and lesson observation is that peer observation is for the benefit of the observer while lesson observations include an element of feedback.)

An additional two teachers have been employed to release teachers from their normal teaching commitments to undertake these observations and coaching sessions, each teacher being entitled to a minimum of eight 1½-hour sessions per year. The role of the additional teachers is not to 'baby-sit' and provide traditional 'cover' lessons, but to deliver a planned learning-to-learn programme.

The simplicity of the input/process relationship

The four-phase lesson plan has transformed my teaching – particularly at A level. In fact, I don't think I have ever approached a lesson the same way again!

Content is a major feature of Post-16 History and it is easy for lessons to be dominated by teaching. Too many of my lessons were simply 'input' sessions followed by a token 'doing' lesson, which usually took the form of a debate.

Now, rather than planning a series of lessons dominated by input, punctuated by an occasional processing lesson, I am much more aware that every lesson needs a processing element. It has just become an automatic way of thinking.

The simplicity of the input/process relationship within a single lesson gives me a framework within which to view:

a) what information is needed in a lesson

b) how we are going to work with it.

This approach has been most valuable not only in the 'role play/debate/presentation' style of lessons (although it has helped achieve more focused and structured preparation for these kinds of activities), but in the more mundane, gritty, unglamorous activities essential for success at A level.

For example, when asking students to take notes, I would often simply give a key question or series of questions to work through for an entire lesson. Since using the four-phase lesson as a framework, I now structure a session as follows:

1 Students have a set period of time to read and highlight the text

2 Students complete a prepared flow-diagram that requires information to be summarised and also shows how each factor relates to the main issue or event

3 Finally the issue or event can be regarded as a whole and the class can then discuss and describe what their diagrams show, allowing them to easily identify the key issue, trends and so on.

Fiona Manser, Tring School

Example: Tring School, Hertfordshire

Rob Edwards, Professional Mentor, Tring School

Context

- 11–18 Secondary School
- NOR 1500

Background

Tring School was involved in the pilot of the KS3 strategy *teaching and learning* in Hertfordshire. Many aspects of the strategy started to be used by some individuals and departments, although this tended to be in isolated pockets, with a lack of consistency across the school. The four-phase lesson plan was adopted as a whole-school policy in September 2002 because it included all the major aspects of the strategy. It also provided a framework for all staff to help them think about their teaching. They were now able to identify the various teaching and learning strategies within each phase and effectively implement them in all lessons.

Impact

The adoption of the four-phase lesson structure has been a major influence on teaching at Tring School. Although it is not expected that staff stick rigidly to the four phases, there is an expectation that that during any observation, drop-in or coaching session, the major elements of learning will be in evidence.

Staff have moved away from thinking just about content and teacher input, to thinking about which strategies can be used to help pupils process and understand the information; they have moved away from thinking about the transfer of knowledge from source to student file, to a more skills- and understanding-based approach.

The template is now embedded as part of normal good practice at Tring. Staff are far more aware of the effectiveness of using different strategies in their teaching and of giving pupils more processing time in lessons. During lessons there is now greater awareness of, and emphasis on, how pupils learn, and learning rather than just teaching.

> *For such a simple idea, the impact of the four-phase lesson template has been huge. It is probably the single most influential thing we have introduced and it provides an easily understood structure for effective lesson delivery across the school.*

Julia Trueman, Headteacher, Tring School

We wanted to base teaching and learning upon a standard template in order to establish a consistency of experience between classrooms. We adopted this particular template because it is both simple and flexible, and crucially focuses explicitly upon learning.

City Academy Bristol

Example: Canterbury Christ Church University – *the Chinese dimension*

Dr Robin Precey, Director Leadership and Management, Canterbury Christ Church University

In 2004, Mr Wang (the Deputy Director of the Yantian Education Bureau in the city of Shenzhen near Hong Kong) decided that he wanted some of the teachers in a bilingual Primary and Secondary school to come to England to both improve their English and further develop their teaching skills, so that upon their return to China they would be able to teach their subjects (Mathematics, Science and ICT) through the medium of English.

A first cohort of six Chinese teachers visited Canterbury Christ Church University from July 2004 to July 2005. During their stay, they looked at both the theory and practice of learning, and spent some considerable time visiting and working in English schools.

It is appropriate to point out that education in China is currently characterised by:

● a great emphasis upon teaching and examination preparation

● great pressure to pass examinations – the culture is fiercely competitive, with examination success being the gateway to university entrance

● teaching that is largely didactic

● students who are generally passive

● class sizes that are extremely large (usually 50 and can be up to 80+)

● teachers operating alone – without Teaching Assistants

● a high degree of centralisation – there is a single science textbook being used across most of the country.

The teachers' experience in China therefore was in sharp contrast to the current emphasis upon learning and active participation by students in UK schools. During their visit, the teachers had studied the four-phase lesson as outlined in *Tweak to Transform* by Mike Hughes (see page 253). This template had proved of interest to the teachers due to its simplicity, flexibility and clear focus upon learning, and was to form the focus for further development when the teachers returned to China at the end of the year.

Their Canterbury tutor visited them in Yantian in October 2005, and was able to observe the teachers at work in their classrooms and to talk to them and their Headteachers about the perceived effects of the exchange programme on their work. It was most noticeable that the four-phase structure was firmly embedded in their teaching and was spreading as good practice throughout the school. Five things, in particular, were apparent:

1 There was an increased emphasis upon sharing aims and objectives at the beginning of the lesson. (This is not common practice in Chinese schools.)

2 There was a much greater focus on learning as opposed to teaching.

3 Students were increasingly active despite the relatively large class sizes.

4 Lessons were broken up into chunks, thus creating multiple beginnings and ends.

5 Teachers were recapping and reviewing at the end of the lesson.

You can be taught to teach, but you have to learn about learning.

Section 4: Unpacking learning

" When teachers learn more about learning, the effectiveness of a school improves.

Chris Watkins, Institute of Education

Many factors impact upon students' learning – levels of motivation, the climate of the classroom, and personal relationships to name but a few. None of these factors should be underestimated and are considered fully in *Closing the Learning Gap* and *Strategies for Closing the Learning Gap* (details on page 253).

In the context of lesson structure, the way in which a lesson is launched and connections are made with prior learning, and the way in which the lesson draws to a close, will significantly affect learning. Indeed, many schools have paid a great deal of attention to the way in which lessons begin and end, and the teacher who cried *Starters and plenaries have been done to death in this school* is by no means a lone voice.

It may therefore be appropriate for schools to focus upon what is happening during the *middle* of the lesson in even greater detail than before, and in particular upon the intricate balance between teaching and learning, transferring information and making sense of it. Both are necessary in the context of the classroom; the significant issue is where the *emphasis* lies between the two. **Is understanding centre-stage?**

Where does the emphasis lie?

One indicator of whether the emphasis of the lesson is on teaching or learning is how long the teacher spends transferring information compared to the time spent helping students make sense of it. As ever, it is a crude distinction.

Extensive lesson observations suggest that:
- there are significant variations between curriculum areas
- there are significant variations between individual teachers
- as a very general rule of thumb, students would appear to spend relatively longer receiving information the older they get
- context plays a part; factors such as top set/bottom set, Tuesday morning/ Friday afternoon, fine weather/windy weather, and so on, all affect classroom practice.

However, context does not account for all of the differences. Two teachers, both teaching convectional rainfall to a bottom set Y9 group in the same school at the same time still may teach in a different way with a significantly different balance of information transfer and helping students understand.

Assessing the teaching–learning balance

Use axes such as those shown below during a lesson observation. Work either individually or collectively. For instructions, see page 109 opposite.

An example is shown below. What does the pattern of this graph tell you about the emphasis of the lesson that has been observed?

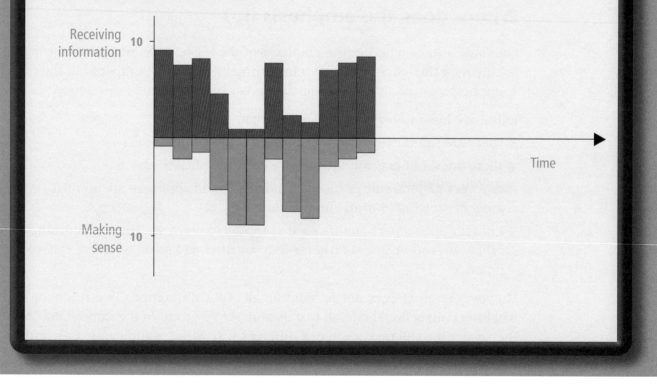

Reflect

- In your lessons, where does the emphasis lie between *transferring information* and *helping students make sense of it*?
- How long do you think you spend transferring information?
- How long do you *really* spend?
- How long do you spend helping students make sense of the information?
- If it depends, what does it depend upon?

The way in which teachers respond to these questions is often based upon their *perception* of what is happening in their classroom. However, there can be a significant difference between what teachers *thought* happened in their lesson and what *actually* took place.

Try this

It was suggested on page 43 that teachers regularly watching themselves teach on video is a potentially powerful catalyst for deep personal reflection, and ultimately change. However, it is all too easy for teachers to see and hear what they are looking and listening for when watching themselves teach. Try the activity outlined below in order to focus attention on the balance between information transfer and understanding.

1 Video yourself teaching.

2 As you play back the lesson, press the pause button every five minutes.

3 Reflect on the five-minute period. Where was the emphasis – on transferring information or on helping students understand it?

4 You have 10 marks to award to reflect that emphasis (for example, receiving information: making sense could be 10:0, 0:10, 5:5, and so on).

5 Record these marks using bars on axes such those shown opposite. Use different colours to increase the visual impact (for example, red = information transfer, blue = making sense).

6 Repeat this exercise for the entire lesson.

Variations

- Complete the graph before you teach the lesson – what do you *think* will happen?
- Complete the graph after the lesson but before you watch the video. What do you *think* happened?

A number of things are significant when you reflect upon your completed graph:

1 How does the actual graph compare to your prediction, or original perception of the lesson?

2 Look at the *relative amounts* of red and blue on the graph. These give a crude indication of where the emphasis lay in the lesson.

continued on page 111

Exercises like these can be the catalyst for professional dialogue ...

... which lies at the heart of professional reflection ...

... which lies at the heart of a *done by* culture.

3 Notice how the *pattern* of the graph reflects the structure of the lesson. For example, a big block of red followed by a big block of blue might indicate that the teacher talked for 20 minutes and then the students were engaged in an activity. This graph would look significantly different to one for a lesson in which the teacher had punctuated short bursts of exposition with quick two-minute reflection exercises. Neither approach is the 'right answer'.

4 When does the first significant (more than 6) blue bar appear? What does this tell you about the way in which the lesson started?

5 What colour, in the main, are the last ten minutes? What does this tell you about the nature of your plenary?

Repeat the entire exercise over a period of time with a number of different groups.

● Does a pattern emerge?

● To what extent is your original graph representative of the way in which you teach?

● Do you notice differences between different groups or situations?

● What do you take away from this exercise?

● What do you do differently as a result?

This exercise can be a significant experience for many teachers. However, although solitary reflection is important, there is also much merit in reflecting with others.

When you are ready to do so, share your video with a colleague. Both of you should complete the graph independently, before comparing your interpretation of events. It is the areas of disagreement that are particularly significant – when you have drawn a mainly red bar (transferring information) and your colleague has recorded the same five minutes as mainly blue (making sense), for example.

By carrying out the activity above, **you have just created the catalyst for professional dialogue ... which lies at the heart of professional reflection ... which lies at the heart of a *done by* culture** (see page 23).

Inevitably, much discussion will focus around *how you know* that the emphasis has switched and that students are now making sense, rather than just receiving information. In short, **how do you know that learning is taking place?** It is the obvious and key question, and lies right at the heart of a national switch in emphasis from teaching to learning. The answer, however, is far from straight forward – learning is a complex and highly individual process.

The rest of this section seeks to unpick the complexity of the learning process and address the question of how you know that students are making sense. It is written in a way to encourage teachers to do the same as they reflect on events in their own classrooms.

The TIMS grid

	Teacher	**Students**
Transfer Information	A	B
Making Sense	D	C

Box A represents the role of the teacher when information is being transferred.

Box B represents the role of the students when information is being transferred – or, from their perspective, received.

Box C represents the role of the students in making sense of the information they have received.

Box D represents the role of the teacher in helping students make sense of the information they have received.

The TIMS Grid

The TIMS grid shown opposite (**T**ransfer **I**nformation **M**aking **S**ense) is an attempt to simplify the complexity of the learning process and break down the many and varied teacher–student and student–student interactions that take place in the classroom. At the outset, it is worth acknowledging that reality is infinitely more complex! The lines on the grid do not exist, or at the very least are hugely blurred. The grid is simply a model and, as with any model, seeks to simplify reality in order to help make sense of it.

The purpose of the TIMS grid is to:
- prompt reflection and discussion, and to deepen our understanding of the way in which learning takes place during lessons
- generate rules of thumb to help teachers during the hurly-burly of the lesson
- generate some concrete indicators that will focus attention during lesson observation
- generate non-judgemental data that will be used for reflection and coaching.

The TIMS grid is based upon the following principles:
- Learning involves receiving information and making sense of it.
- In the classroom, we have the teacher and other adults and a group of students.
- The teacher is primarily, but not exclusively, responsible for introducing and transferring new information.
- The teacher is then responsible for helping students make sense of the information.

Try this

Work in small groups (4–6) to fill in the grid. We are not looking for the *right* answer; we are seeking to generate discussion and reflection in order to deepen our understanding of learning and our role in the process.

Box A What is the role of the teacher when information is being transferred? What is the teacher most likely to be doing? How would you recognise this in the classroom?

Box B What is the role of the students when information is being transferred – or, from their perspective, received? What are they most likely to be doing at this stage? How would you recognise this in the classroom?

Box C How do you know when the emphasis switches from students receiving information to making sense of it? What are students most likely to be doing at this stage? How would you recognise it in the classroom? How do you know that *learning* is taking place?

Box D What is the role of the teacher when the emphasis switches to students making sense of information? What do teachers do to help students make sense? How would you recognise it in the classroom? How do you know the teacher is *facilitating learning*?

Example: Waingels College, Reading – *making sense of making sense*

Andy Love, Leader, Teaching Development Faculty, and Science AST

● 11–18 Mixed Comprehensive.

● NOR 1600

● specialist in Maths and Computing

● Waingels is a successful school. Examination results are high and the majority of lessons were graded 'good' during the last OFSTED inspection.

Background

One of the outcomes of the TLR reforms was the creation of a Teaching Development Faculty (TDF). This consists of five members of staff who hold key whole-school responsibilities in teaching and learning (AfL, ICT, thinking skills, training school and foundation curriculum). A key part of the brief was to turn good lessons into great ones. The Teaching and Learning Development Faculty works closely with the Teaching and Learning Club (TALC) which is a group of enthusiastic staff who meet voluntarily every half term.

Focus

Our initial focus is on 'making sense'. The rationale is simple: if we want to see more learning taking place in lessons, we have to tweak the balance between students receiving information and making sense of it.

Action

1   The Teaching Development Faculty worked closely with Mike Hughes to develop a clear under standing of what making sense 'looks like'. Central to this is the notion that students must do something with the information they receive in order to make personal sense of it. We refer to these internally as *The Magenta Principles* (see the list on page 153).

2   Members of the TDF observed each other teach. During these observations we completed a version of the graph on page 108 to both establish a picture of what was happening in our classrooms and generate further discussion.

3   At a staff meeting we:

    ● shared the Magenta Principles with the staff

    ● showed a 15-minute video clip of a lesson taught by one of the members of the TDF. Staff worked in groups to complete the graph on page 108.

Continued on page 116

Two things to be aware of:

1 When asked to consider the questions at the bottom of page 113, many teachers are tempted to say, *it depends – learning is complex!* It quite probably does depend. However, the whole purpose of the exercise is to attempt to unpick complexity and this answer can be used a catalyst for reflection and discussion. What does it depend on? Does the role of the teacher in facilitating understanding change when trying to help younger or older students, top sets or bottom, and so on? Does the role of the teacher in helping students make sense differ in various curriculum areas? Are there generic principles that can be identified?

2 Many teachers are tempted to use fairly general words and phrases to complete the grid. For example, words like *facilitate* and *scaffold* often appear in box D. Answers like these can also be used as a springboard for further discussion. What do they mean? How do you know a teacher is facilitating learning? What does that look like in the classroom? What is the difference between facilitating learning and telling students what to do?

A variation

So much of what teachers do in the classroom is intuitive. This is particularly true when we are trying to help students understand something. The way in which we intend to transfer information (box A) can be planned in advance; our response to a question or misconception (box D) is often based on a spur of the moment, intuitive decision.

Keep a copy of the blank grid on your desk. When you next help a student or group of students through a blockage or deal with a misconception reflect on *precisely* what you did. Almost certainly, you have facilitated learning; what, *specifically*, did you do? Keep a record over a period of time and share your views with your colleagues. We are trying to articulate the intuitive and isolate the specific strategies so many teachers use almost sub-consciously. When we are conscious of the strategies that we – and others – use in the classroom, we can arguably use them even more effectively.

> *In many respects, adults are just like children, and if we want teachers to be learners and deepen their understanding they have to be given the opportunities to explore and discuss. Just like children, they need a focus and framework to work in. Tools like the TIMS grid provide such a framework and can spark such interesting and powerful discussions. These discussions can lead to real learning taking place – and, crucially, improvements to practice.*

Sue Kershaw, Headteacher, Gorse Hill Infant School, Swindon

Waingel's College – continued from page 114

The intention was to both raise awareness and to generate discussion. On both counts, it was a spectacular success.

Comments from staff included:

- *This approach has enabled us to have such positive and non-judgmental discussions.*

- *It has made me think about how much actual learning goes on in my classroom. It has also given me the strategies that I can use to tweak what I already do and increase the learning that goes on.*

- *These tools really open your eyes to what is happening in your classroom. You can't help but go straight out and try them out.*

- *I have found all of this work inspirational – I just wish that I'd had it earlier in my career.*

- *When you've been teaching for years it's hard to find a new way of looking at things. These approaches help you see what's really going on and give you simple but powerful ways of helping students to make sense.*

- *This is a very powerful, deep reflective tool.*

- *This experience is going to make me reflect differently on my lesson planning.*

- *Using the TIMS framework has depersonalised the reflection with colleagues and made the resultant discussion non-judgmental, leading to a more productive and focused review of the practice.*

The last word goes to Ruth Evans, the Co-Principal:

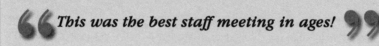 *This was the best staff meeting in ages!*

Unpacking the boxes

In order to further our understanding of learning, it is necessary to unpack the boxes of the TIMS grid. A number of things are apparent:

1 People have to unpack them for themselves! You have to learn about learning, rather than being taught about it. Therefore, although some suggestions are made, the emphasis here is on promoting reflection, enquiry and discussion.

2 We are working in a context where the majority of teaching is already of a high standard. Even so, we are striving to improve still further, as it is the quality of teaching which holds the key to the quality of learning, which in turn will determine levels of achievement. This demands that we search the boxes for *excellence* rather than *competence*. Most teachers know what 'good' looks like – do we know what constitutes 'great'?

3 As we've already acknowledged, reality is, of course, infinitely more complex than the neat, regular grid on page 112. The TIMS grid is simply an attempt to break down the undoubted complexity of the learning process and draw attention to the distinction between receiving information and making sense of it, between knowing and understanding. It involves reflecting at a metacognitive level on what so many teachers do instinctively and intuitively.

What follows is therefore offered as no more than food for thought, and as suggested rules of thumb. The limitations of such generalisations are acknowledged in advance; however, it is precisely because learning is complex and messy, and classrooms are such frenetic places, that teachers can benefit from unambiguous guidelines such as these.

> *Our focus for the last few years has been trying to establish where teaching stops and learning begins. We have had many fascinating staff discussions around this theme; often they have been sparked by watching videos of ourselves teaching. We have also employed some of the tools outlined in this book; they too have prompted deep personal reflection and debate.*
>
> *There is no doubt that our collective understanding of learning grows ever more sophisticated. There is equally no doubt that the adjustments that we have made to our teaching as a result of this process have led to significantly enhanced learning taking place.*
>
> Sue Dodd, Headteacher, Y Bont Faen Primary School

Knowing / understanding

Diagram A

transfer information → receive information → recall and reproduce information = knowing

Boxes A and B on the TIMS grid are essentially about information – the outcome is **knowing**.

Diagram B

develop understanding ⟷ demonstrate understanding

assess understanding

Boxes C and D on the TIMS grid are essentially about making sense – the outcome is **understanding**.

Above the midline (boxes A and B)

The boxes above the horizontal midline of the TIMS grid (boxes A and B) are essentially to do with **information**. They represent the *transfer and test* approach that characterised the classroom for a great many years, with the teacher's role as little more than 'vessel filler'. The outcome of a successful transfer of information is **knowing**. When testing – formal and informal – reveals that the procedure was unsuccessful and that the information cannot be recalled and accurately reproduced, the process is repeated.

Fundamentally, this is a linear process – as represented by diagram A, opposite. The diagram neatly illustrates what is often referred to as *shallow* or *surface learning*. It has its place – there are times when you simply need to know – but it is a limited and limiting concept of the learning process. The problem arguably arises when boxes A and B exist in isolation and there is no activity below the midline. Boxes A and B are necessary – but whereas once they were deemed sufficient, now they are increasingly viewed as just the starting point.

Below the midline (boxes C and D)

The boxes below the horizontal midline (C and D) are essentially to do with **understanding**. They represent a deeper process – often referred to as *deep learning*. Below the midline, the responsibility of the teacher expands considerably from transferring information and checking if it has been received, to developing and assessing understanding. Many would describe this process as facilitating learning.

Facilitating deep learning is an infinitely more challenging and complex process than telling and checking. Indeed, it is a process that defies a linear illustration, for the three major components are tightly interwoven (diagram B, opposite).

- If making sense of information is the goal of the classroom, teachers have to give students ample opportunities to both develop and demonstrate their understanding. The two are inextricably linked as the act of demonstrating understanding will inevitably help develop it.

- In a similar way, when students demonstrate their understanding, they give the teacher the opportunity to assess their current picture of the world and to identify any misunderstandings and blockages. It is only when teachers can accurately assess students' current level of understanding that they can help them develop it further.

If boxes A and B are essentially to do with **knowing** and boxes C and D are fundamentally about **understanding**, it follows that all teachers have to be clear about the difference.

> **Reflect**
>
> - What is the difference between knowing and understanding?
> - How do you know that someone understands?

The TIMS grid

	Teacher	Students
Transfer Information	A	B
Making Sense	D	C

Box A is about telling, demonstrating, instructing and showing.

It is what, for many years, was generally regarded to be teaching.

Boxes A and B (See page 112)

Box A is about telling, demonstrating, instructing and showing. Often, exposition is punctuated by a series of low-level closed questions, designed to check if information has been received.

Resources include books, artefacts, ICT, pictures, diagrams, and so on. The teacher and indeed the students are also potential and significant sources of information.

Box B is to do with seeing, hearing, feeling and – to a lesser degree in school learning – smelling and tasting. Although information comes from a huge range of sources – teachers, fellow students, videos, books, diagrams, maps – it can only be received through the five senses.

Box A

Five things are worthy of note in box A. Information should be transferred:
1 in a variety of ways
2 in chunks
3 with clarity and accuracy
4 in a way that sometimes doesn't make sense
5 in a way that captures imagination and stimulates curiosity.

1 Variety of ways

There are at least three reasons why it is often beneficial to transfer information in a variety of ways:

● People prefer to receive information in different ways.

● Activating different senses increases the chances of recall.

● Transferring information in different ways maintains interest.

People prefer to receive information in different ways

The fact that the whole issue of learning styles is so often oversimplified and exaggerated – the vast majority of students are not 'visual' or 'auditory' learners but *multi-sensory* learners – should not be allowed to detract from the basic principle that people prefer to receive information in different ways. Although for some people it is slight, for others the preference is most marked.

Put simply, transferring information in a variety of ways offers no guarantees, but makes it more likely that more students on more occasions will receive information in a way that will ultimately make sense to them.

Eric Jensen argues that teachers are only 'reaching' between 60 and 80% of students at any given time. He goes on to suggest that the difference between an average teacher and a great teacher is that the average teacher reaches the *same* 60–80% all the time while the great teacher reaches a *different* 60–80% on a regular basis.

Primacy and recency effects

The primacy and recency effects suggest that, in general, concentration and recall are greatest at the beginning and end of an experience. Put simply, lessons with multiple beginnings are therefore likely to be more effective than those with lots of 'middle'.

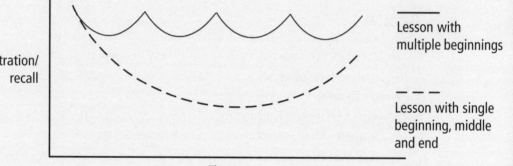

Beginnings can be created:

- by including more than one activity
- by punctuating a longer activity with mini breaks – for example, pause to set homework, or to reflect on progress so far.

Capturing the structure of a lesson

When observing a lesson, use a simple timeline to record precisely what happens. Use specific symbols to mark events – for example, ‖ = new activity, / = mini break – and make notes about activities, levels of concentration, and so on.

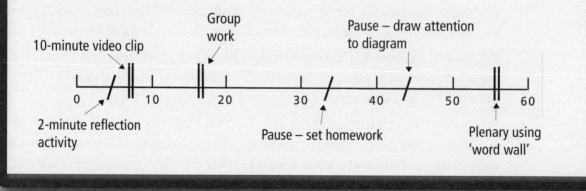

Activating different senses increases the chances of recall

Different sensory memories are stored in different parts of the brain. In crude terms, the more ways information goes in, the more places it is stored and the greater the chance it will be retrieved eventually. Indeed, deliberately engaging all five senses is a common 'memory technique'.

Transferring information in different ways maintains interest

Enough said!

2 In chunks

> There are at least two reasons for exposing students to new information in chunks:
> ● to provide processing time
> ● to create beginnings.

To provide processing time

Receiving and making sense of information is a little like eating and digesting food. We eat a meal and allow time to digest it, before eating another one. Even our meals consist of separate courses punctuated by a short break to aid digestion.

The brain operates in much the same way, receiving information and then processing it. Too much information too quickly and the brain has difficulty in making sense of the new inputs. The brain is almost saying, *Stop! Shut up for a while and let me deal with this stuff – then feed me some more.* For while the brain is processing and consolidating a new input, further information simply gets in the way.

This processing, which happens both consciously and subconsciously, best takes place during what is often referred to as *downtime* – a period of no further external input, to give the brain a chance to sort itself out. This is why many educationalists recommend punctuating lessons with short periods of downtime or *timeouts*. Many argue that just a couple of minutes every fifteen or twenty minutes (slightly longer and more frequently when the new material is particularly complex) help the brain digest new information.

To create beginnings

Concentration is often greater at the beginning of an experience than in the middle. Certainly, recall is often greater at the beginning and end of an experience (though this is not to suggest that learning is solely about memory). This is known as the *primacy* and *recency* effect.

Lessons that consist of a single activity lasting around 40 minutes have just one beginning and lots of 'middle'. Punctuating a lesson with mini breaks creates a series of beginnings and ends. This could of course involve organising lessons around two or three discrete activities, or simply punctuating a solitary task with a couple of timeouts. (Ideas for timeouts can be found in *Strategies for Closing the Learning Gap* pages 41-3, and 57. For details see page 253).

There's little point in giving students 'ready-made meaning'.

Paul Ginnis

3 With clarity and accuracy

Exposition has long been one of the stock tools of the teacher's trade, with the ability to explain something in simple terms the hallmark of a good teacher. In some respects, nothing has changed; there are times when a simple and concise explanation from the teacher is both necessary and highly effective.

However, as Paul Ginnis points out (opposite), teachers cannot *give* students understanding, only information, and it raises the fascinating question of whether the teacher's role is to make things simple or make things hard.

4 In a way that sometimes doesn't make sense

Although there are times when the appropriate strategy is to simplify things for students and to provide a clear, unambiguous explanation, there are also times when it can be effective to deliberately present information in a way that doesn't make obvious and immediate sense.

Eric Jensen suggests that *Only when we are stopped in our tracks by a problem or situation and forced to rethink it is there the possibility of new learning.* He also argues that *Suspense, surprise, disequilibrium, uncertainty and disorder can lead to a richer understanding of the content.* Put simply, when teachers deliberately present information that doesn't at first appear to make sense, they invite the student to think things through again, and so deepen their understanding. This process is often referred to as **cognitive conflict** and forms the backbone of many thinking skills programmes.

When teachers simplify information, they are effectively trying to provide students with the answer, and make sense for them. However, when they present information that doesn't fit immediately into the students' existing picture of the world, they present students with a puzzle, and – by helping them solve it – enable them to make sense for themselves, so deepening their understanding.

Put another way, students have an existing mental map of the world and their brain is in a state of equilibrium. By deliberately creating some confusion, the teacher throws the brain into a state of disequilibrium. Learning occurs as the student gradually accommodates the puzzling information into their world and restores equilibrium in the brain.

A key component in this process is the support that the teacher provides in helping students reach this new state of equilibrium (box D), for, as Philip Adey and Michael Shayer point out, *Students and adults confronted with evidence which they find difficult to explain often produce a series of irrational or self-contradictory statements in an attempt to 'explain away' the evidence without fully engaging with it.*

Learning is triggered and sustained by curiosity.

John West-Burnham

It is also important that the teacher does not create *too much* confusion. We are seeking to present information that doesn't *quite* add up, rather than content that is completely incomprehensible. For when students feel that new information doesn't make *any* sense, they are highly unlikely to engage with it.

There is a great deal of consensus that deep, meaningful learning is a messy, complex and unpredictable process. It is somewhat ironic, then, that mainstream policy in recent years has been to 'tidy' and standardise teaching! Of course, there are occasions when it is appropriate and effective for teachers to give students the complete picture, yet we know that **individuals only truly make meaning when they 'join the dots' for themselves**.

> **Reflect**
> - Is the teacher's role to make things simple or to make things hard?
> - Where is the emphasis in your lessons – giving students the complete picture or helping them join the dots?

5 In a way that captures imagination and stimulates curiosity

Consider the following. Which of the two scenarios is most likely to arouse your interest and stimulate curiosity?

> **A** You are watching the TV when you notice your next-door neighbour leaving her house. You glance at the clock; it is 3.00 pm. There is nothing unusual in this as your neighbour leaves her house every weekday at 3.00 pm to pick up her children from school. It all makes sense and you continue to watch the TV undistracted.
>
> **B** You are watching the TV at 11.00 am when you notice a Rolls Royce pull up on your neighbour's drive. Two men dressed in formal dark suits get out and ring the door bell. Without waiting for a reply they return to the car. Within a minute, your neighbour leaves her house and gets into the back of the car. You notice that she is wearing a formal grey suit and carrying a small package. As she enters the car, no words or smiles ar exchanged. It is most unusual – your neighbour is the quiet type who rarely goes out.

It is highly likely that it is scenario B that would arouse your curiosity, simply because the episode was unusual and couldn't be easily explained. In other words, it did not make immediate and obvious sense.

Deliberately transferring information that does not quite add up does more than create confusion and conflict in the brain, it triggers curiosity. This in turn leads to students who are listening and reading because they *want* to find out, rather than because they have been told to. It is a significant difference! (See the case study described on page 207.)

Intrinsic and extrinsic motivation

Issue a group of students with a pro forma such as the one below.

Group _____   **Male/Female**

Write down a number that accurately reflects your mood right now.

I'm doing this because ...

I want to   **I have to**

10   9   8   7   6   5   4   3   2   1   0

Sample 1 _____

Sample 2 _____

Sample 3 _____

(10 = I really want to, 0 = I have to, 5 = a bit of both, 7 = mainly because I want to, and so on)

Simply stop the lesson a couple of times – for example, near the beginning, halfway through and again near the end – and ask students to record their scores.

You can calculate an average score, average for boys or girls, and so on. These scores can be recorded on axes such as those shown below.

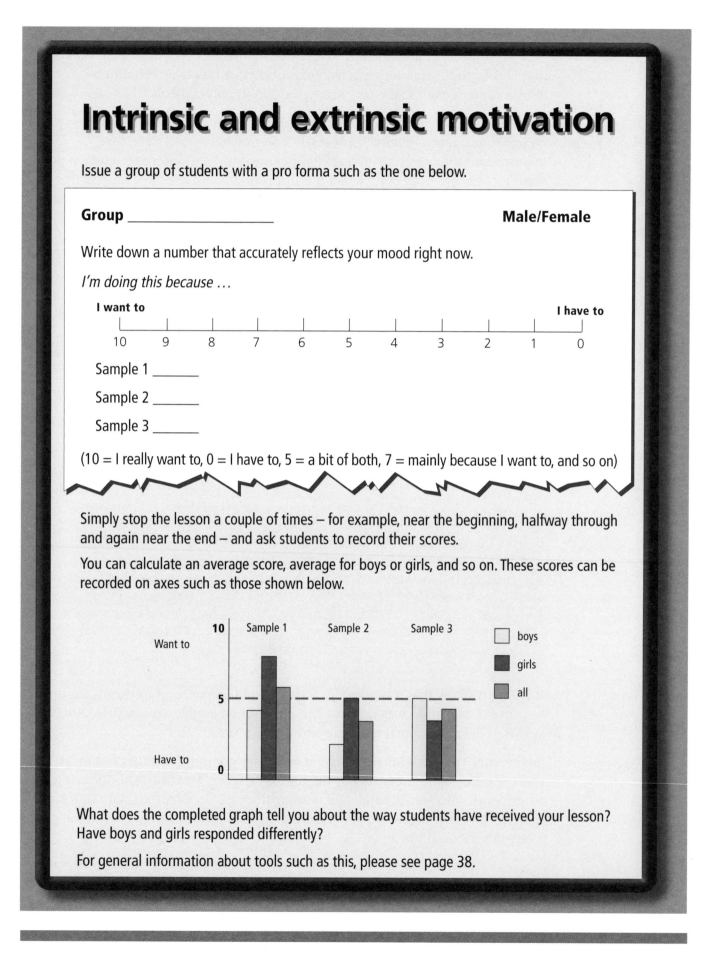

What does the completed graph tell you about the way students have received your lesson? Have boys and girls responded differently?

For general information about tools such as this, please see page 38.

Box B (see page 112)

> Two things are of significance in box B.
>
> 1 Are students receiving information because they *want* to, or because they *have* to?
>
> 2 Do students recognise significant information when they receive it?

1 Want to / have to

Box B involves students receiving information by reading, listening, watching, and so on. At least, this is what they are supposed to be doing!

Those that are listening, reading or watching are doing so because they:

1 think that they *have* to, because if they don't they will get into trouble – they wish to avoid detention

2 think that they *need* to, because the topic may come up in the exam

3 genuinely *want* to find out more.

1 and 2 are about *extrinsic motivation*, while 3 involves learning for its own sake – *intrinsic motivation*. There are, of course, variations around this theme, but the fundamental principle that at any moment in time students who are paying attention are either extrinsically or intrinsically motivated remains.

It goes without saying that most teachers would prefer to teach a group of intrinsically motivated students listening because they are genuinely intrigued and want to find out more. Equally, most would prefer teaching extrinsically motivated students rather than be faced with a group of students who are misbehaving and not listening at all!

Motivation belongs to the individual. Some students are fascinated by a certain topic – for example, space – and any lesson involving this issue will inevitably capture their imagination, irrespective of how it is taught. All teachers have taught students who share their love of a subject. The real challenge is, and always has been, how to stimulate a student who does not possess an inherent interest for whatever particular topic is being covered.

There are no guarantees, but it is more likely that students will be listening because they want to when:

● they are curious – which, in turn, is more likely when they are puzzled (page 207)

● when they are seeking information to answer a question that they themselves have posed (see page 149).

> **Reflect**
>
> Consider a lesson that you taught recently. Were students listening, reading or watching because they:
>
> ● felt they *had* to
>
> ● felt they *needed* to
>
> ● genuinely *wanted* to find out more?
>
> Try the exercise opposite – be warned, it can make pretty depressing reading!

Triggering the Reticular Activating System is a bit like setting a fly trap. It simply means that the information entering the brain will be more likely to stick.

2 Recognising significant information

You have the radio on in the background and are 'listening' to a weather forecast for Europe while you go about your business. Information is given about snow conditions in the Alps. The information – which has no personal relevance – goes in one ear and straight out of the other. In other words, it is received and instantly discarded. It would be a very different story if you were just about to embark on a skiing holiday to the region!

This is an example of the **Reticular Activating System** (RAS) at work. We are constantly bombarded with literally millions of pieces of information per second and so have an internal filter device in the brain – the Reticular Activating System – to ensure that we only pay conscious attention to that which is deemed relevant and important to us at any given moment. Consequently, we are significantly more likely to see and hear information that we are looking and listening for.

Students receive huge amounts of information every day and the last thing we want is for it to go in one ear and out of the other. However, this is precisely what will happen if the brain does not recognise incoming information as significant. Although the information will be received, it will be immediately discarded – unless the brain knows that it is important to hold on to.

So it is vital that teachers consciously trigger the Reticular Activating System – in effect, they are setting the flytrap so that the information, once received, will be more likely to stick.

> There are a number of ways that teachers can increase the chances of significant information being recognised as such. These include:
>
> ● ensuring that students know what they are looking for during a lesson
>
> ● basing lessons around key points
>
> ● placing task before content
>
> ● encouraging students to ask the questions.

Ensuring that students know what to look for

This is most usually done at the beginning of the lesson, or the beginning of a particular phase of the lesson, and is often linked to the sharing of learning objectives. Much depends on the language of the teacher; in effect, we are talking directly to the brain and telling it what to notice. For example:

● *While you are watching the video clip, keep your eyes open for three factors which influenced ...*

● *During today's lesson, you will notice anything to do with ...*

● *As you are reading the passage, you will notice three reasons why ...*

● *During the discussion, listen carefully for any connections between ...*

● *As we go through chapter one, be on the alert for any clues that suggest the character is violent.*

In your teaching, figure out what are the two or three key points for the lesson, the unit or month. Keep referring to those, post them and weave them into your discussion every chance you get. These will become like the center of a spider's web to attract other information and create meaning.

Eric Jensen

Basing lessons around key points

What would you cover if your lesson lasted just 60 seconds? If you could wave a magic wand and guarantee that all of your students remembered just one thing from your lesson, what would that one thing be? Almost certainly, you would cover – and want your students to remember – the *key points* of your lesson. These are the facts or concepts that need to be stressed, repeated and covered in more than one way during the time available.

Eric Jensen argues that teachers should constantly be emphasising and referring to the key points during a lesson or unit of work (opposite). Effectively, these key points act like magnets or hooks – Jensen likens them to the centre of a spider's web – and are used to attract other information, which in turn is used to create meaning.

Placing task before content

When task follows content ...

... students do not know *why* they are watching. The Reticular Activating System has not been triggered and it is possible that key information may be missed simply because the brain wasn't looking for it.

When the task is described before the content is presented ...

... the RAS has been alerted. Students are now watching for a purpose.

Encouraging students to ask the questions

Actively encouraging, even requiring, students to ask questions has many learning benefits. Not least is the general rule of thumb that people are more likely to be on the lookout for and notice information that is the answer to a question. This is particularly true when the question has been generated by the student rather than imposed by the teacher. Some strategies for encouraging students to generate questions can be found on page 149.

The TIMS grid

	Teacher	Students
Transfer Information	A	B
Making Sense	D	C

Box C represents the role of the students in making sense of the information they have received.

Box D represents the role of the teacher in helping students make sense of the information they have received.

This part of the TIMS grid is essentially about **understanding**.

Boxes C and D

While all four boxes in the TIMS grid (page 112) are clearly inextricably linked, it is particularly difficult to view boxes C and D in isolation.

> The following section is based upon these principles:
>
> **1** Boxes C and D are essentially about understanding.
>
> **2** Meaningful learning takes place at the next level.
>
> **3** Students can go further with help.

1 Understanding

 Understanding is a primary goal of education.

DfES

There is little doubt that understanding is central to learning. If this is true – and we accept one of the key messages of this book, namely that the more we know about learning, the better able we are to facilitate it in others – there is a strong argument that teachers need to develop a deeper understanding of understanding.

A useful starting point is to explore the difference between **knowing** (boxes A and B) and **understanding** (boxes C and D). The exercise could form the basis of a profitable Professional Reflection Day.

There are, of course, no easy answers. For whereas it is possible to move from a state of not knowing to knowing simply by receiving the necessary information, understanding is infinitely more complex.

Three issues are worth highlighting:

● **There are degrees of understanding.** You can possess anything from a tentative grasp of a subject to in-depth understanding of it.

● **Understanding is personal.** Christopher Bowring-Carr and John West-Burnham contend that *understanding is a matter of the creation of personal mental maps or models, the creation of one's reality.* Thus understanding, unlike knowing, can vary between people. Two people may well both understand something but their personal mental maps can never be identical.

● **Understanding can develop.** Mental maps or understanding can change as the individual interacts with, and responds to, fresh experience and more information. A person may understand an issue but ten years later – although they still understand it – their understanding will have changed. In this sense, understanding only exists for a moment in time.

Let us view understanding not as a state of possession, but as one of enablement. When we understand something, we not only possess certain information about it but are enabled to do certain things with that knowledge.

David Perkins

David Perkins, in his excellent book *Smart Schools* (see page 251 for details), suggests that *understanding is a multilayered thing* and, while knowing is a state of **possession**, understanding is one of **enablement**. Perkins argues that *when we understand something, we not only possess certain information about it but are enabled to do certain things with that knowledge.* Or, in Jerome Bruner's words, *the person who understands is capable of going beyond the information given.*

This means that there are certain things that an individual can do to demonstrate that they have made the transition from knowing to understanding. Perkins refers to these things as ***understanding performances,*** and suggests the following as examples:

- explaining something in your own words
- giving new examples
- applying new knowledge or skills to different situations
- justifying something by offering evidence
- comparing and contrasting with other situations
- contextualising the knowledge.

It's also possible to add:

- creating a metaphor (see page 73)
- recognising when something doesn't add up and make sense – in other words, knowing when something is wrong.

These understanding performances give us a clear indication of the kinds of activities that help develop understanding. For demonstrating and developing understanding are inextricably linked.

Reflect

- To what extent to you agree with the list of *understanding performances* above?
- What would you wish to add to it?
- To what extent to you give students the opportunity to demonstrate these *understanding performances*?
- Re-visit the exercise on page 119. What is the difference between knowing and understanding?

Gauging the level of challenge

The following procedure was adopted by Tom Dore, at Waingels College in Reading (see page 114), to build up a picture of what was taking place in his classroom. Students were given a form like the one below and asked to indicate how challenged they felt at various stages throughout the lesson.

Male/Female

How challenged are you feeling by this lesson right now?

Is this lesson really making you think?
Is it really hard? Or
Is it soooooooooo easy it's no challenge at all?

When your teacher asks you, rate how challenged you're feeling at that precise moment by giving it a score between 0 and 10.

0 = *So easy my baby brother could do it.*

10 = *My brain is hurting I'm having to think so hard.*

Lesson Date	Time into lesson (mins)						
	0	10	20	30	40	50	60
1							
2							
3							

This procedure was used by a Year 8 top set over a period of 5 lessons. The average results were illuminating.

	Minutes into lesson						
	0	10	20	30	40	50	60
Boys (15)	0.5	3.18	3.67	4.40	4.80	4.10	5
Girls (10)	2.79	3.77	3.46	3.75	5.05	3.2	-

> *Even though my lessons are judged to be good, I am always looking for ways to improve. The messages from this exercise were unequivocal: not only did students report a general lack of challenge; they were clearly telling me that they didn't feel any significant challenge until the second half of the lesson.*
>
> *This exercise, and the other work that we have done within the Teaching Development Faculty, has been fascinating and has enabled me to reflect upon my teaching in a non-threatened way. In particular it has:*
>
> *1 made me think carefully about how much learning actually goes on in my classroom*
> *2 given me clear strategies that I can use to improve learning*
> *3 given me the confidence to try out new approaches.*

Tom Dore, Waingels College

2 Meaningful learning takes place at the next level

Learning involves an element of progress – knowing, understanding and being able to do something that previously you could not. This means that teachers have to engage students at the 'next level'.

In crude terms, if a student is at 'level 3' she has to be working at 'level 4' in order to progress; 'level 2' is too easy, 'level 3' is stagnation (this is different to consolidation) while 'level 8' is over-optimistic. Few would argue that getting the level of challenge right for each student is a key challenge for the teacher. When work is too easy, students become bored; when work is perceived as impossibly hard, they switch off (see pages 41 and 141).

This concept is best illustrated by Vygotsky's *Zone of Proximal Development* (ZPD). This is the area just in advance of a student's current level of understanding. It is where things are tricky, challenging and puzzling – but not impossible. This is the zone in which students would struggle if working in isolation – but represents a level at which they can operate with help.

3 Students can go further with help

Vygotsky's ZPD represents a level of challenge that students can meet with help. This assistance is often referred to as *scaffolding,* and comes from the teacher and from the student's peers. Learning occurs as the scaffolding is gradually removed – less help is provided – so that the student can do unaided what previously he could only manage with assistance.

Reflect

If we accept that meaningful learning takes place in the *zone of challenge* (page 140), the following questions become relevant:

- On a scale of 1 to 10, how challenging are your lessons?
- If the answer is, *It depends*, what does it depend upon?
- How would the students respond to the first question? How would the most able student respond? How would the least able student respond?
- How long do students spend in the challenge zone in your lessons?
- How quickly do you take them to the challenge zone at the beginning of the lesson?
- What is the nature of the support that students receive from their peers when they are operating in the challenge zone?
- What is the nature of the support provided by you, the teacher, when your students are operating in the challenge zone?
- How do you ensure that levels of support are gradually removed so that individual students can progress from working with assistance to working unaided?

The Zone of Challenge

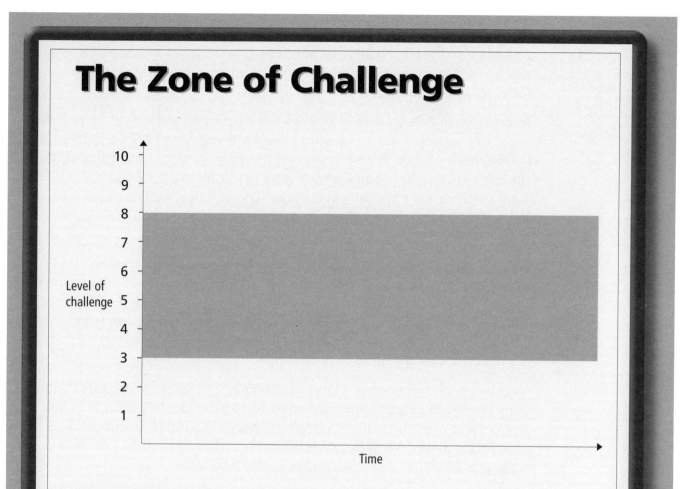

Procedure:

On a scale of 1–10, consider the level of challenge for students, during every 30-second interval throughout the lesson. Record your feelings on the axes.

The scale:

Use 1–3 when you consider the activities to be too easy, and 8–10 when tasks are too difficult. (The intention is not to put a 'glass ceiling' on learning, but simply to acknowledge that people cannot learn too far in advance of their current level of understanding.) Thus there is a *zone of challenge* (between 3 and 8, shaded above) in which children are being stretched and challenged without finding the work impossibly difficult.

Consider the graph opposite. Classroom activities are graded for the level of challenge on a scale of 1–10. Levels 1–3 are considered to be easy – too easy for learning to take place. Levels 8–10 are considered too hard, given the students' current level of understanding. This creates a *zone of challenge* – the shaded area on the graph.

The graph is designed to:

● help teachers reflect on the questions on page 139

● provide a visual representation of what is happening in a lesson

● create non-judgemental data

● offer food for thought.

For further information see page 38.

Try this

1 Watch a video recording of yourself teaching a lesson.

2 Every 30 seconds throughout the lesson, consider to what extent students are being challenged. (Use longer intervals if you prefer.) Record your thoughts on a copy of the axes opposite with a cross.

3 Revisit the questions on page 139.

4 Complete the exercise for a series of lessons with different groups.

5 Does a pattern emerge?

6 If you have carried out the exercise on page 108, how does the blue/red graph you created then compare with the information generated by this exercise?

7 What do you take away from these exercises?

An example of how this Zone of Challenge graph has been used in practice is shown on page 40.

Note:

● This exercise can be completed for the group or for an individual student. When considering the group, it is important to remember that each student's zone of challenge will fall in a slightly different place. The graph provides no more than an approximate snapshot.

● This tool works best when the exercise is repeated a number of times. We are trying to establish if patterns emerge.

● The scale does not seek to impose a 'glass-ceiling' on challenge and achievement. Rather, it acknowledges that students cannot work too far in advance of their current understanding.

Learning is when you take in what the teacher – or your friends – are telling you.

That's not learning though, that's listening. It's only learning if you think about it.

Ben, aged 9

Box C (see page 112)

Box C is where the emphasis switches and students begin to make sense of the information they have encountered. This is the place where learning – certainly deep learning – takes place.

David Perkins argues that *learning is the consequence of thinking*. Ben (opposite) would appear to agree. Together they suggest that listening, watching and generally receiving information is insufficient to promote learning. **In order to understand information, you have to do something with it, at least at a cognitive level.**

Although this book has acknowledged that there is no single correct way to teach because there is no single correct way to learn, it may be possible to establish some general rules of thumb to guide our practice in the classroom. The following are therefore offered as no more than suggested guidelines.

> Teachers can significantly increase the chances of students understanding something when they encourage them to:
>
> 1 **verbalise** their thinking
>
> 2 **ask** questions
>
> 3 **do something** with the information they encounter
>
> 4 **reflect** on what they have learned and how they learned it.

Two further dimensions are also worth highlighting:

- Students should be given significant *choice* in how they both develop and demonstrate their understanding (see page 177).

- Developing understanding – learning – is not a one-off activity; learning involves a significant *'re'* element (*re*visiting, *re*-thinking, *re*-drafting, and so on – see page 179).

Reflect
- How do you respond to the list above?
- What would you wish to add to it?
- How does this list compare with what takes place in your classroom?

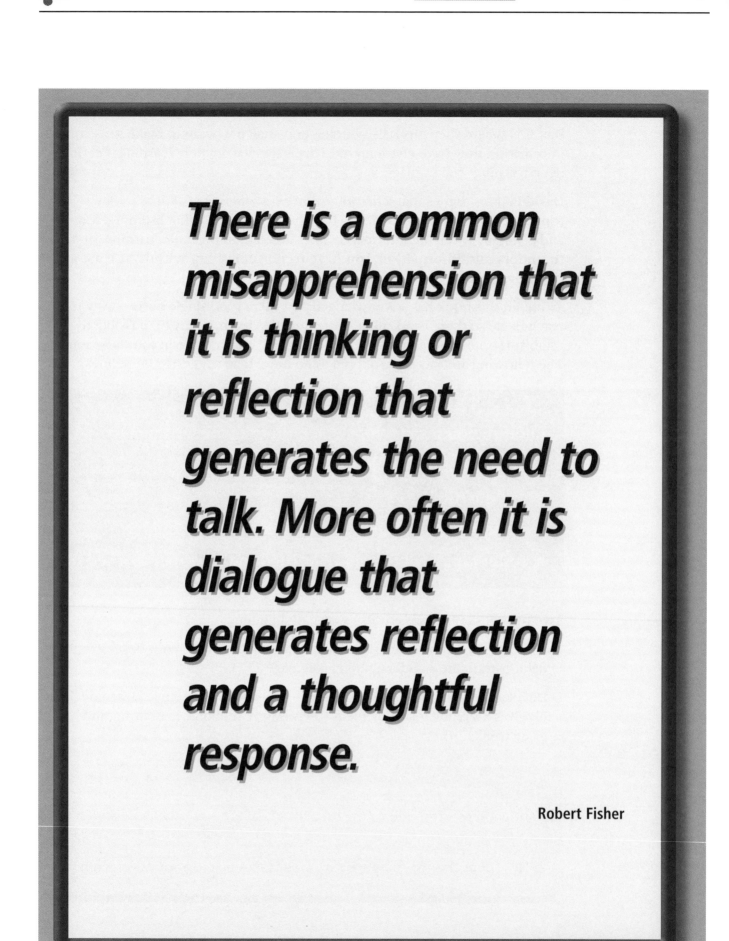

There is a common misapprehension that it is thinking or reflection that generates the need to talk. More often it is dialogue that generates reflection and a thoughtful response.

Robert Fisher

1 Verbalise

There is an old adage – *if you want to know a subject, teach it.* As with so many similar pearls of wisdom, there is more than an element of truth in it. Indeed, many would suggest that you retain as much as 95% of what you teach, compared with around 10–20% of what you read and hear.

However, the benefits of explaining are not confined to recall. Win Wenger argues that *what you express is 10 to 100 times more productive of your learning than what is expressed to you.* In other words, it is talking rather than listening that develops understanding.

Even if the figures quoted above are treated as guidelines rather than absolutes, there is still a clear message that talking is a key to learning. Ask someone to explain something. Then ask that person to explain it again. The second explanation will almost certainly be richer, more detailed and more coherent that the first, simply because the process of articulating your thinking helps the brain to organise its thoughts. It is a strategy frequently employed by the police and coaches alike.

Talking is more than evidence of what a person thinks, it is a technique that can be consciously used to help someone think through and clarify an issue in their mind. The implications for the classroom are clear; we want to encourage students to talk about their learning. This is in stark contrast to the classroom of a few years ago, when teachers were often judged on their ability to keep students quiet!

As a general rule of thumb, we need to be taking every opportunity to **encourage students to talk about their learning**. These opportunities include formal 'report back to the group' sessions, and more informal talk. For example:

- *Jenny was away last week – can you tell her three things we learned.*
- *Read page 17 and decide which you think is the most important sentence. Tell the person sitting next to you which you have chosen, and why.*
- *You have 30 seconds to talk with the person sitting next to you before deciding on your answer.*
- *In your group, decide on just one word from the list. Remember, you have to reach a group decision.*
- *Explain your diagram to your partner.*

Variations around the talking theme include the following:

- Describing something aloud as you are doing it. This includes anything from, *I'm putting a semi-colon here because …*, *I'm doing the bit in brackets first …*, *I'm playing this shot with a firm wrist …*, and so on. This technique of describing something aloud as you do it is often referred to as ***pole-bridging*** – a phrase coined by Win Wenger.

If I know something, I can tell you in the teacher's words.

But if I understand it, I can tell you in my own words.

Alix, aged 8

- Describing something aloud as someone else is doing it – a teacher, fellow student, or person on a video, for example. This technique is often called *commentary*.

- Describing or explaining something as if to a blind or deaf person. For example, students might watch a video clip showing the biodiversity of a tropical rain forest and then describe what they have seen to a blind person. (This could also be a written exercise.) Having to communicate their own visual experience to a person who cannot see at all will sharpen students' observation and result in a much richer, more detailed description. This in turn will help to deepen understanding.

- Describing or explaining something to someone two years younger. This forces the learner to *simplify* information and is one of the reasons why teaching something is such a powerful learning strategy in its own right.

- Sharing disparate pieces of information as a group, and putting them together in order to make meaning. For example, in groups of 3–6, each student could be given an isolated piece of information (a photograph, diagram, fact or set of notes, for instance). In this way, nobody has the complete picture and the only way that the group can construct meaning and make sense of the topic is to share their information. However, they are not allowed to show people their information – only talk. (A really good example of this technique can be found in *The Teacher's Toolkit* by Paul Ginnis, page 179.)

Of course the reality of many classrooms is that when students are invited to talk about their learning, they talk about anything but! Two simple ideas to increase the chances of students talking and listening about the topic in hand are described below.

1 Student A begins explaining something. In the middle of the explanation, select a second student at random. The second student must continue the explanation – from precisely the point at which the first student finished. Students are much more likely to be paying attention when they know they could be selected at any moment. Referred to as a *chain explanation*, this is a technique that can easily be taught to a group of students of any age.

2 Invite students to spend 30 seconds discussing something with their partners. Then add that one pair will be selected at random to summarise their discussion to the rest of the class.

Reflect
- Where is the emphasis in your classroom – on students talking or listening?
- What is the balance between teacher and learner talk?
- Is this the same for all groups?

You can tell whether a man is clever by his answers.

You can tell whether a man is wise by his questions.

Naguib Mahfouz, Nobel Prize winner

2 Asking questions

The desire to ask questions is innate in human beings. Babies ask questions of their environment before they can talk and walk. Spend anytime around young children and you cannot fail to notice that they are inquisitive and full of questions – answers simply being the catalyst for the next question. Enter any key stage 1 classroom and notice how children are posing questions; enter any secondary classroom and notice how students are answering them. Of course, this is a generalisation, but it contains more than an element of truth.

Maybe the tendency to stop asking questions is an inevitable part of growing up, maybe it has something to do with peer pressure, and maybe it is the way we teach students in the formal world of education. Whatever the cause, there is a strong argument that teachers have a responsibility to protect and fan the flame of curiosity that burns so brightly in infants or, if has already been extinguished, to re-ignite it. In many respects, encouraging students to ask questions is about establishing – or sustaining – good learning habits; for asking questions is fundamental to learning, and the ability and inclination to do so are characteristics of an effective learner.

Asking questions stems from curiosity and the desire to find out. However, the relationship between curiosity and asking questions is two-way:

- people ask questions when they are curious
- asking questions can lead to curiosity.

There are a number of ways of encouraging the learner to ask the questions – a few suggestions are listed below. All of these techniques can be used in a variety of ways – for example, questions can be generated by individuals or groups of students.

- Model good learning behaviour – ask questions yourself.
- Display key questions around the wall (*Where ...?, Why ...?, When ...?, Who ...?, What ...?,* and so on).
- Frame lessons or learning experiences in the form of open questions (see page 41).
- 'Reduce the risk' by allowing students to generate questions in pairs or small groups.
- Have a question box so that students can drop their questions in anonymously.
- Allocate an area of the classroom as a 'question wall' where students can post questions.
- Give assessment marks for the quality of the questions, not the answers.
- Have a 'question of the week' award.

An effective rule of thumb is to require students to ask at least one question about any new information they receive. For example:

"We are now going to listen to an archive recording describing life as an evacuee during the Second World War. Afterwards, each group has to ask two questions about it".

This simple technique will almost certainly increase concentration levels.

● Generate questions as a group at the beginning of a unit of work (*What do we already know about …? What would we like to know about …? How might we find out …?*) – the group could even write the end-of-module test at the beginning of the module: *We now have the next four weeks to find out the answers.* (See the example on page 234.)

● Tell students that during the next lesson there will be a visit from a famous author, artist, scientist, athlete, historical figure or expert of some kind (as appropriate). Ask students (alone or in groups) to identify two questions that they would like to ask the visitor. They must explain why they think their questions are important. The following lesson, a student or teacher can 'hot seat' as the visitor, and answer the questions in role.

● Alternatively, students (alone or in groups) could generate 10 possible questions and then select the 'best' two.

● Ask students to demonstrate an event or concept in the form of a frieze. Other students are then able to bring an individual from the scene to life by touching that person on the shoulder and asking a question.

● Students can ask questions as a basis for taking notes. Before they read a passage, they identify the questions that they wish to answer and write these at the top of a page as column headings. They then read each sentence or paragraph in turn – if it provides the answer to any of the questions, they note down the information in the appropriate column.

● Punctuate a demonstration or period of exposition by saying, *Normally I would ask a question now – can you think what I might ask?* Alternatively, ring a bell – every time the bell goes, all students have to ask a question.

● An effective rule of thumb is to require students to ask at least one question about any new information they receive. For example, *We are now going to listen to an archive recording describing life as an evacuee during the Second World War. Afterwards, each group has to ask two questions about it.* This simple technique will almost certainly increase concentration levels.

● Extend this by encouraging students to pose questions *before* they receive the information. Follow up by discussing which of their questions were answered and which were left unanswered, and identifying any new questions that need to be asked in the light of the new information.

Reflect

● What is the balance between teacher-generated and learner-generated questions in your classroom?

● What strategies do you consciously employ to encourage students to ask questions?

● What do you give marks for during assessment – the quality of questions or the quality of answers?

Irrespective of differences in age, ability and subject, one general principle holds true: in order to make sense of information you must do more than simply receive and reproduce it – you have to do something to it.

3 Do something to the information

David Perkins' *understanding performances* (page 137) are a useful starting point. Perkins argues that the ability to do certain things with information indicates a movement from knowing to understanding. This ability, however, is more than just evidence that a student understands, as the process of *demonstrating* understanding will simultaneously help to develop it. Thus the list of understanding performances suggested on page 137 becomes a handy guide for effective activities to foster learning in the classroom. For example, while the ability to compare and contrast information *indicates* understanding, engaging students in the process helps to *deepen* it.

There are any number of things that you can do to information, and the precise nature of the strategies that are used in the classroom depends on variables such as age, current level of understanding and the nature of the subject area. However, one general principle holds true: **in order to make sense of information you must do more than simply receive and reproduce it – you have to do something to it**.

For example, you can:

- reduce it
- change it
- assemble it
- search for it
- connect it
- arrange it
- enlarge it

- simplify it
- classify it
- compare it
- contrast it
- de-construct it
- apply it
- prioritise it …

And so on. These actions – which can be used in combination – can be incorporated into concrete strategies, adapted to suit the particular circumstances of the students and subject area involved. The examples that follow illustrate some ways in which such actions can form the basis of effective learning activities. (This list is referred to as *The Magenta Principles* by the staff at Waingels College, Reading. See page 114.)

Reflect

Consider the list above.

- What would you wish to add to it?
- To what extent does the list reflect practice in your classroom?

Reducing information comes in many guises – including prioritising, imposing limits and rank ordering. In all cases, however, students are faced with a dilemma and need to make a decision.

As with many of these strategies, the follow-up questions to reveal the thinking behind the decision are crucial.

Reduce information

Reducing information is arguably the most useful strategy of all in the classroom. Not only is it an exceptionally effective learning strategy in its own right, it is highly flexible, requires little preparation and is quick to implement. As with so many techniques for 'doing something' with information, it can be effective to start with students working individually or in pairs, and then move to small groups and finally work as a whole class. Some examples of activities involving reducing information are described below.

- *Here are 20 calculations – do the three hardest ones.*

- Reduce a passage of text to just one page, paragraph or sentence, or even to a single key word! Alternatively, identify the single most *interesting* word, or perhaps the six most important words in the passage.

- Reduce a diagram to the most important word, or key section.

- Reduce a story, play or account by identifying the key character, event or turning point.

- *You have been asked to cut a whole scene from Macbeth for television purposes – which scene do you cut so that the meaning of the play is not lost?*

- Impose a limit: *Prepare and deliver a 40-second report on this event ... Summarise this article in 150 words ...* (Then reduce the limit again to 30 seconds, or 110 words, for example.)

- A4 limit: *Summarise this topic on a sheet of A4. (If you were allowed to take just this sheet into your exam, what would you write?)*

- Reduce a piece of text by removing a word at a time – without altering the meaning. Students work in groups of three. Two people remove words while the third acts as a referee. The first person to remove a word that alters the meaning of the text significantly loses the game. (This is particularly effective with young children.)

- Identify the key strength of a well-known sporting personality's skill (for example, Federer's backhand, or Wilkinson's goal kicking).

- Place information in rank order, according to a certain criterion – for example, in order of importance, or influence, or interest. This is a form of reduction as a large number of ideas are effectively reduced down to the one most significant. An alternative is to 'pyramid rank' the items (identifying the most significant, followed by the two next most significant, with three at the next level, four at the next, and so on) or arrange them in a 'diamond nine' (where information is laid out in a 1–2–3–2–1 diamond formation – see page 166).

- Reduce, Reduce, Reduce! Repeated reductions are very powerful. For example, reduce a paragraph down to eight key words. Reduce it again to just four key words. Finally, reduce it down to one key word. Begin by working in pairs and move up to a whole-class discussion.

Activities in which students *reproduce* information involve *knowing* and *remembering*.

Activities in which students *re-construct* or *change* the form of information develop *understanding*.

So, as a simple rule of thumb:

In order to demonstrate and develop understanding, ask students to convert information to a different form.

- Where is the emphasis in your classroom – on students reproducing or re-creating information?

Change information

Along with reduction, changing the form of information – re-creating it – is one of the most useful learning strategies for the classroom. Not only is it very powerful, it is also easy to prepare and quick to implement.

Five things are worthy of note:

1 **Learning involves constructing meaning.** Activities that require students to change the form of information are based upon *re-constructing* information. They are fundamentally different to activities that require students to *reproduce* information – which have more to do with knowing and remembering, than understanding. A simple rule of thumb for the classroom is therefore to require students to convert the information they encounter into a different form.

2 A spin-off benefit of the 'changing information' strategy is that it **increases the chances of allowing students to learn in their preferred learning style.** When students are asked to change a piece of text into a mime, students with strong kinesthetic tendencies benefit. When the activity requires a topic to be summarised in a song, students who are particularly musical benefit, and so on.

3 **Students can be given a choice** (see page 177). The choice can be open: *How would you like to change this?* Or guided: *Would you like to show me this as a flow diagram or a cartoon strip?* (How many linear, sequential thinkers would plump for the flow diagram?)

4 **Changing information can be used in conjunction with other strategies.** For example: *Reduce 'Romeo and Juliet' to three key moments or turning points. Show these events as visual images – or physical gestures – or both.*

5 It is important to **ask students to explain their thinking** and, when appropriate, justify their decisions. For example: *Having portrayed the turning points of 'Romeo and Juliet' as images, describe your images and explain the thinking behind them to your partner.*

Examples of activities involving changing information include the following:

- Describe (orally or in writing) a visual source of information, such as a graph, diagram, model or photograph.
- Turn a written description into a diagram.
- Convert text into a flow diagram or cartoon strip.
- Convert a piece of text, a diagram or a process into a play, mime or frieze.
- Put key words to music, or write a jingle.
- Use key words to write a poem.
- Paint a piece of music.
- Visualise a piece of text – describe your visualisation.

Drawing is a wonderful way of making thinking visible. A child may not find it easy to express thinking in words but can always attempt to express it visually.

Robert Fisher

- Take the key ideas from a story, event or explanation and create a visual image for each. These can then be converted into a physical action, gesture or mime. This works best when students are encouraged to explain what their images and gestures mean.

- Turn a story or a play into a line graph, tracing the highs and lows of a theme. For example: *Trace the theme of prejudice in 'Romeo and Juliet'*.

- Turn an explanation or piece of text into a 'model'. This can be as simple as asking students to show their understanding using just the things lying around their desks: *Show me your understanding of how a volcano erupts. You can use your desks, things on your desk and any items of your uniform that can be easily removed (tie, jumper, and so on)*.

  An alternative is to construct a more elaborate model using pre-prepared resources. For example, students could turn a map into a model (using sand for deserts, stones for mountains, and so on). If one group makes a model of Africa and another does South America, for example, they can then swap and turn the other group's model back into a map.

- Mime a poem.

- Convert a movement (a tennis serve, for example) into six still frames.

- *We are producing the Walt Disney version of Hamlet (like the Robin Hood version featuring a fox as Robin Hood) – your task is to cast the play. Which animal do you choose to play each character and why?*

- Create a metaphor or analogy to explain a topic or issue (see page 73). Teachers often use analogies in teaching: *It's a bit like* … Use the prompt, *It's a bit like* … and get the students to finish it off.

Assemble information

This approach is based upon the principle that if learning involves constructing meaning, students have to build up, or assemble, their understanding of an issue or concept. Although there are many variations, the key principle behind this strategy is that, during an activity, *not all* of the information necessary for understanding is:

- given in one go
- given to any one person
- given in the same way
- given in a completed form.

The following are examples of activities requiring students to assemble information:

- Cut maps or diagrams to create jigsaw puzzles. Students work individually or collectively to create the picture. A variation is to complete the exercise 'blind'. The student who is constructing the picture is not allowed to see the pieces – these must be described by other members of the group.

The Coffee Mystery

There are many coffee growers in north west Tanzania. Two of them are Sangito and Abel. In the late Autumn of 2000, one of them was arrested by the police and fined a large amount of money. Your task in this mystery is to find out who was arrested and why.

Work in groups of 4–6. Distribute the 'clue' cards (below and overleaf) evenly among the group. You are allowed to tell others in your group what's on your cards, but not show them.

Names: _____

First thought and findings: _____

The landscape around Sangito and Abel's coffee trees is forest, which grows well in the warm and wet conditions of this part of Tanzania.

Sangito grows coffee in the land around his house in north west Tanzania. All the family work on the farm, including his wife and their three children.

Sangito and Abel sell the coffee beans that they grow to a cooperative. This is a business that gathers together the crop of about 50 farmers and then sells it all together for a better price. The profits are shared among the farmers.

Abel is also a coffee grower. He lives on the land next door to Sangito's farm. He lives alone and looks after the coffee trees around his home on his own.

Abel has no close family living nearby. His parents, brothers and sisters moved away to the city two years ago to start a new life.

The amount of rain in north west Tanzania is increasing every year.

Abel grows about 200 kg of coffee in one year, which earns him £42. That's 21p for every kilogram of coffee he grows.

Sangito grows about 400 kg of coffee in one year, which earns him and his family £84. That's 21 pence per kilogram.

Sangito earns about £7 a month from the coffee that he sells to the cooperative. This is the equivalent to two days' food for the family.

There is no social security system or unemployment benefit in Tanzania to help support people and families.

In his spare time, Sangito fixes Landrovers to earn a bit of extra cash.

Abel earns £4 a month from the coffee that he sells to the cooperative. This is the equivalent to one day's food for a family.

- Each student in the group is given some information. Students are not allowed to show it to anyone else but they are allowed to describe it orally. The group must work together to construct the 'whole picture' - solve a problem, timeline an event or draw a conclusion, for example. In essence, this approach is *social meaning making* and therefore mirrors much of what we know about learning. The 'Coffee Mystery' on pages 160 and 162 is such an example.

- Share information. (This activity is often referred to as *snowballing*.) *In pairs, think of three possible reasons why ...* Pairs join - *Now see if you can get five reasons between you.* Finish as a whole class - *Together can we get 10 ?*

- Work in groups, with each group responsible for researching a different aspect of the overall topic. Groups then collaborate to assemble the big picture.

- Provide information from a variety of sources. For example, transfer some information orally, provide some information through text, some in the form of a diagram, and so on.

- Provide information gradually throughout the lesson, or over a series of lessons. This approach is particularly effective when students are explicitly encouraged to connect the discrete pieces of information - see page 163.

- Assemble meaning. Give each student in a group the same piece of information, and ask them to look at it from different perspectives. For example, within each group, ask every student to consider a story from the perspective of a particular character, or to consider a particular question relating to the story. Then, within the class as a whole, all the students who are focusing on a specific character or question are given ten minutes to meet and discuss their particular issue. Afterwards, students return to their original groups, and discuss the story from their various points of view, putting together their disparate perspectives to create a deeper understanding of the whole.

Search for information

All of the examples suggested so far involve students being *given* information. Any of them could of course be adapted to require students to first *search* for information, before then doing something with it. Searching for information can involve anything from a major research project to identifying facts within a short passage of text. (For example: *Have a look at the first two pages, and see if you can discover three pieces of information about the cottage.*)

All teachers have experienced students collecting large amounts of information that has simply been copied from a book or printed off from the internet. Episodes such as these rarely lead to any significant learning and the important thing is not how *much* information can be collected but what is *done* with it.

Information that has been collected can then of course be reduced, changed, prioritised, arranged, and so on. Searching can also be combined easily with assembling information by asking each student in a group to research just one aspect of the topic being studied. Students can then share their various pieces of the information jigsaw in order to build up a complete picture.

The Coffee Mystery (continued)

The average price that people in Britain pay for 1 kg of ground coffee is £9. That's £8.79 more than Sangito or Abel is paid for growing the coffee beans.

The coffee that Abel and Sangito sell to the cooperative is then sold on to large multinational companies in Europe, North America and Australia.

Global warming has meant that the weather in certain parts of the world has become either wetter or drier.

By late autumn 2000, Sangito's family are finding it harder to buy food. They cannot grow food on the land they have because it has coffee trees planted on it. They are all beginning to despair.

Human beings are changing the world's climate by putting more carbon dioxide (CO_2) into the atmosphere. This means that more heat from the Sun is absorbed, which leads to global warming.

It is illegal to cut down trees in forested areas in Tanzania. This law was brought in to prevent deforestation.

The large multinational companies in Europe, North America and Australia take the raw coffee beans and process them into ground coffee powder and instant coffee granules.

The price of coffee all over the world fell in 2000. This was because coffee growers in South America had a good crop, and so there was more coffee for sale.

It is very difficult for companies in Tanzania to process coffee beans to make ground coffee and instant coffee to sell into Europe, North America and Australia.

In late autumn 2000, Abel gave up on the coffee farm, packed his things and left to join the rest of his family in the city.

There was an unusually wet summer in 2000 in the coffee growing area of north west Tanzania. This meant that many of the coffee growers had a bad crop.

Abel had a pest infestation and all of his coffee trees became ill. This meant that they did not produce fruit.

Many of the people living in the coffee growing areas of north west Tanzania do not get 2100 calories in their diet each day. This means that they are malnourished and get ill more easily.

In a rage, Abel burned down his coffee tress in late autumn 2000.

Some governments in Europe, North America and Australia put tax on ground coffee and instant coffee made in other countries. The tax on coffee beans is very low.

Most of the CO_2 released into the air each year comes from more wealthy countries like the USA, Japan and the UK, where fossil fuels (coal, gas, oil) are consumed and burned.

The large multinational companies in Europe, North America and Australia make a large profit from selling coffee.

An average adult human needs about 2100 calories in food each day to remain healthy.

This exercise was developed by Douglas Greig, Thomas Tallis School.

Connect information

Connecting information lies at the heart of understanding. An effective strategy for the classroom, therefore, is to make connecting explicit. The following strategies can be completed individually or collaboratively. The experience is often more powerful when carried out in groups, as this maximises the opportunities for students to verbalise their thinking.

- Known as **connections**, this strategy begins by presenting students with two pieces of information, in any form – text, diagrams, facts, photographs, graphs, and so on. Students have to explain how the two pieces of information are connected. Introduce a third piece of information. Students must now consider if their initial connection is still valid or if it needs to be revised. Continue to add new pieces of information as the lesson progresses and invite students to consider if their connection still holds true. This works best when the information comes in a variety of forms and when the early pieces of information could clearly be connected in more than one way.

- This is a variation on the *odd-one-out* theme. **Odd-one-out** is a well known and highly effective strategy in many thinking skills programmes. Students are presented with a number of pieces of information and asked to identify which is the odd one out. Again, this works best when there is more than one valid answer.

- **Dominoes** involves presenting students with a range of information – facts, pictures, diagrams, maps, and so on – on small cards. Students work in small groups (3–6) and the cards are distributed equally. The first player lays a card and the second player must lay one of their cards next to it. In orthodox dominoes, you are only permitted to lay a domino if the numbers match; in this version, you are only allowed to lay a card if you can connect the information on your card to the information on the card that has just been laid in some way. Other players are allowed to challenge the connection if they feel it is bogus.

- **Link the clues** is another variation. Provide students with a series of clues in the form of additional information. See how quickly they grasp what is going on – or how few clues they require.

For example, the process of freeze–thaw weathering involves water freezing in cracks in the rock when the temperature drops below 0 °C. When water turns to ice, it expands, thus enlarging the crack. When this process is repeated many times, the rock begins to weaken and eventually splinters.

This information could be presented to students in the form of separate clues that can be pieced together to identify the link – the more information they receive, the easier it becomes. For example, present students with the following two clues:

1 Ice occupies a larger volume than water.

2 Rocks in upland areas are often splintered and shattered (show photograph).

Making connections

As a lesson starter, I used heart-shaped sticky notes and put on words linked to having a healthy heart. A sticky note was attached to each student as the class entered the room and I 'left them to it' during registration.

Some interesting conversations arose. Some students naturally looked for a word that connected with their own – such as HEART and BEAT – and discussed the meanings or prepared an explanation. Other students were able to explain all the facts they knew about a healthy heart using what they saw on other students as prompts.

A variation is for students to write down all the linked words they see and discuss them with their talk partners.

Penny Stevens, AST, Deansbrook Junior School, Mill Hill.

Few students will completely grasp the process of freeze-thaw weathering from such limited information. However, it may well be sufficient to stimulate some discussion and speculation - not to mention generate a degree of curiosity (see pages 207–217). Add a third clue:

3 The temperature in upland areas often drops below freezing – particularly at night.

Follow with a fourth:

4 The temperature in upland areas frequently rises above freezing – particularly during the day.

And a fifth, sixth, and so on, as required:

5 Any water in cracks in the rock will freeze when the temperature drops below zero.

6 Ice will melt when the temperature rises above freezing.

7 As ice occupies a larger volume of water, water turning to ice will expand and the crack will be enlarged.

8 When the ice melts the water will trickle down further into the enlarged crack.

9 This process will be repeated many times.

● Sticky notes are a useful tool for helping students make connections. The activity described opposite shows one way in which this strategy can be implemented in the classroom. However, the generic principle can be adapted to a multitude of situations.

 Understanding is related to the ability to make valid connections between existing knowledge and experiences with that of new inputs.

John Abbott

Diamond Nine

Take time on a professional reflection day to consider **the most significant influences on learning in the classroom.**

Work in small groups (3–6) and arrange the statements below in a diamond formation. The statement that you collectively believe to be the most significant should be placed at the top, while the least significant influence (in relative terms) is placed at the bottom. Statements placed on the same line indicate that you have attached equal significance to them.

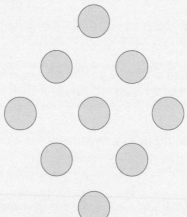

1 Treating children as individuals

2 Getting the level of challenge right

3 Children generating their own questions

4 Children regularly reflecting on what and how they have learned

5 Children being active

6 Immediate feedback

7 Talking

8 Clarity of learning objectives

9 Smiling

Arrange information

The process of arranging information, particularly when done collaboratively, is an effective way of helping students explore an issue, while their final arrangement provides the teacher with a clear indication of how students are thinking. Again, there are multiple variations around the theme and although the strategies below have been grouped under the heading *Arrange information*, they also involve students *prioritising, reducing* and *connecting*.

As with all of the approaches in this section, it is important to encourage students to explain the thinking behind the patterns they create.

- This exercise can be done individually, in pairs or as a whole class. Identify a topic – for example, *Reasons why Britain and the Allies won the Second World War*. Write the topic title in the middle of a piece of flipchart paper. Either give or encourage students to generate a number of factors and pieces of information related to the topic – for example, *bulldog spirit, winning the air war, the entry of USA, Hitler's failure to invade post Dunkirk*, and so on. Students then arrange the facts on the paper:

  1 in a way that shows how the discrete pieces of information relate to each other

  2 in a way that shows the relative importance of each factor – those considered to be the most important are placed nearest to the centre of the page.

- Mind maps are another effective way of helping students clarify and demonstrate their thinking. Essentially, creating a mind map involves students arranging and connecting their thoughts. Mind maps are most usually drawn but they can also be created from physical objects to produce a mind map model. Highly kinaesthetic!

- A 'diamond nine' exercise is arguably the most effective way of generating thought and discussion in the classroom. It is highly engaging, very flexible and a particularly useful way for starting or ending a unit of work. Students are given nine statements about a particular topic. (An alternative is to allow students to generate some or all of the statements for themselves.) They then arrange the statements in the form of a diamond (see opposite), placing the statement they believe to be the most important or significant at the top of the diamond, with the statement they believe to be the least significant at the bottom. Statements placed along the same horizontal line have equal significance.

  The teacher can either place a strict time limit on the exercise, or allow the discussion to run its course.

  An effective way of organising this exercise is to ask students to have a go on their own at first, and then to combine ideas with a partner. Pairs can then join to form small groups, which finally come together to construct a whole-class diamond. Guaranteed to generate discussion!

It may look similar, but there is the most fundamental difference between:

A *"Read page 7."*

and

B *"Have a look at page 7, and tell me which you think is the most important sentence."*

Children are simply receiving information in scenario **A**.

But in scenario **B** they have to do something to it.

● Sequencing information is a variation on the 'arranging' theme. One way of organising this approach is to cut a piece of text into segments. Then ask a group of students to stand in a row at the front of the class, and give each student a section of the text. Make sure that the text is distributed at random. Working along the line, ask each student in turn to read aloud their piece of text – it will make little or no sense as the order has been jumbled. The rest of the class then has to organise the text so that it makes sense, by directing the students to change positions. For example: *I think Jenny needs to move nearer the beginning of the line* or *I think Tim should be sitting next to Phil.* Get the newly sequenced students to re-read their pieces of text – the account should now make more sense. Repeat the process until the class is happy that the information makes sense. This technique can be adapted for anything from poems to quadratic equations.

● Asking students to classify is another method of getting them to arrange information. The classification categories to be used could either be provided by the teacher, or identified by the students, and the students then arrange the information accordingly. Create confusion and controversy to stimulate discussion by including information that doesn't fit easily into any category, or that could fit into more than one.

General

1 The examples suggested over the last few pages are by no means exhaustive and illustrate only some of the principles suggested on page 153.

2 All of the tasks outlined here are designed to allow the student to both *develop* and *demonstrate* their understanding. In this way, the teacher can *assess* whether the student understands rather than simply knows something (see page 118).

3 It is important to give students frequent opportunities to justify their decisions and explain the thinking behind their actions.

4 The tasks are designed to provide plenty of opportunities for both student-student and teacher-student interaction (talking) (see page 145).

5 The tasks can be done individually or collaboratively. There are clearly times when it is necessary to ask students to work alone; however, the simple task of selecting the most important sentence on a page becomes a potentially more powerful learning experience when done in pairs, in a small group or even as a whole class.

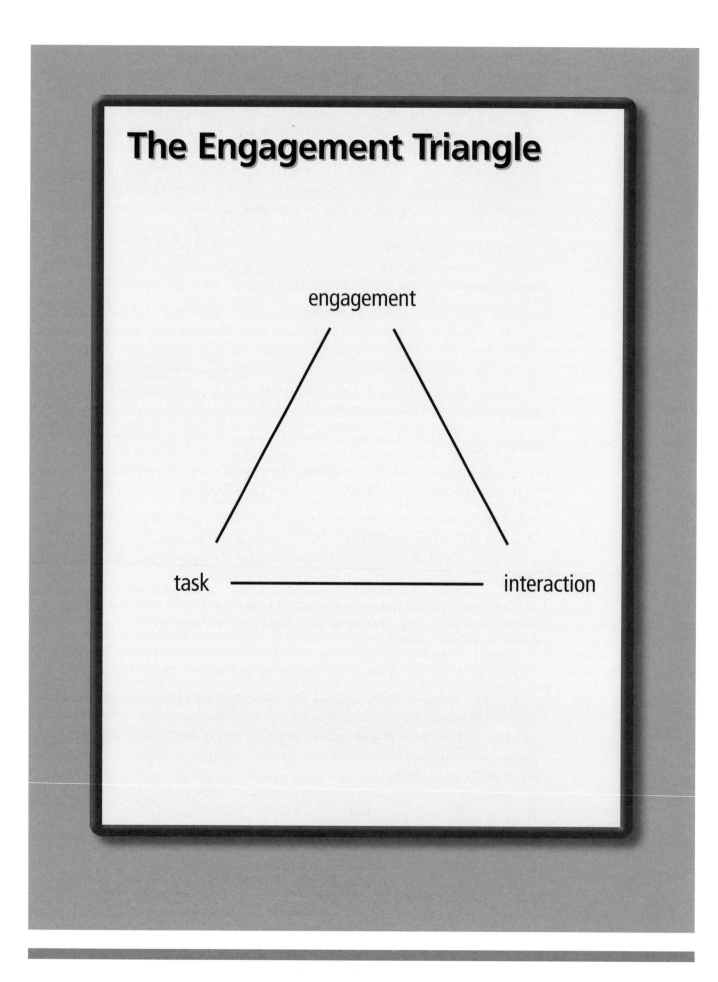

The Engagement Triangle

Engagement = Task + Interaction

Teachers aim to engage students during lessons – for learning is an active process, in which the individual makes meaning. This engagement is the result of both the tasks set by the teacher and the ensuing interaction between learners. Indeed, the tasks outlined on the previous few pages have one thing in common: all are designed to be the catalyst for *interaction*. Interaction in this context simply refers to talking and questioning – taking place in learning situations in pairs, small groups or as a whole class – and includes both student–student and teacher–students exchanges.

This relationship can be shown in the diagram opposite – the *Engagement Triangle*.

> **Reflect**
>
> ● Which do you think is more important, the task or the interaction?
> ● Why?

Both the task and the associated interaction are clearly significant in the learning process. Indeed, the reflection exercise above is a reduction or prioritising activity, simply designed to prompt reflection and generate discussion.

However, consider the points below.

● If the key factor in learning *was* the task:

1 the leadership challenge would be one of simple dissemination to ensure that all teachers know about the best tasks

2 all learning experiences based upon the same task would be of equal quality.

● Yet this is clearly not the case. There are many excellent tasks that are widely available to teachers. Many of the thinking skills programmes such as *CASE* (*Cognitive Acceleration through Science Education*) and the *Thinking Through* series (Geography, History, English, and so on) are based upon high quality tasks that are designed to create a degree of confusion (cognitive conflict – see page 221) in the brain and allow students to think through an issue for themselves. Many excellent lessons are based around such tasks. However, there are also any number of lacklustre lessons that are also taught – even though they have been based upon the same tasks. This would suggest that it is not the task alone that leads to learning, but the way the task is used by the teacher and the interaction it generates. Indeed, it could be argued that the task is, or at least could be, the constant while the variable – the *key* variable – is the interaction.

While the task provides the catalyst and the context, the real learning is done through talking and interacting with others.

The quality of tasks has improved significantly during the last decade – now is the time to refine and develop the way in which we use them.

● Education has finally cottoned on to the fact that good ideas have to be shared among the profession. However, the vast majority of ideas that are shared are to do with tasks. This is not surprising – it is easier to disseminate information about tasks and activities, as they are tangible; they can be written down, collated and physically swapped outside of the lesson, at a meeting or on a training day. Interaction – questioning and talking – takes place in the lesson, and cannot so easily be pinned down.

● Many would argue that, while the task provides the catalyst and the context, the real learning is done through talking and interacting with others. Two points are worth making here:

   1 As a sweeping generalisation, some teachers are better at managing this aspect of the learning process than others.

   2 This is too significant an issue to be left to chance.

● **Schools have a simple choice: consider issues consciously and collectively, or leave them to chance.** Interaction is one of those issues that requires collective attention. For many schools and teachers, this represents the next step. The quality and range of tasks has improved significantly in many classrooms during the last decade – now is the time to apply the polish, and refine and develop the way in which we use them.

● One final point: teachers can be given tasks and told how to use them; the issue of improving interaction demands a different approach. For while guidance can be provided, teachers have to *learn* about interaction, and they do this by enquiring, noticing, reflecting and discussing. All schools use vehicles to provide an impetus for improvement – for example, *Assessment for Learning and/or Thinking Skills* was used by many schools as a focus that led to changes and improvements in practice. A whole-school focus on the quality of interaction in the classroom has the potential to be used in a similar way.

Reflect

If you believe that the quality of interaction is a highly significant factor in determining the quality of learning in the classroom:

● what do you do about it?

● what could you do about it?

The profession has finally accepted that learning is an active process. Consequently, we find far more pupil activity during lessons than ever before.

The next step in the challenge to enhance learning in the classroom is to convince teachers that reflection is a key ingredient in the learning process.

We must not let words like metacognition deter us; we simply need to make thinking conscious by regularly inviting children to consider both what and how they have learned.

4 Reflection

On page 89, attention was drawn to the facts that:

- reflection plays a central role in the learning process
- reflecting on learning helps learners develop an understanding of learning and thus creates better learners
- better learners learn better.

It was also suggested that reflection is the component of learning most likely to be neglected – squeezed out as the pressure mounts to cover the syllabus and deliver the curriculum.

Teachers are always on the lookout for ideas to improve learning in their classroom. It appears some are searching for the Holy Grail – the answer is out there somewhere, if only they could find it. They attend courses, read books and buy products to this end. Yet there are no magic answers, no product or scheme – however well packaged or cleverly labelled – that will miraculously and dramatically improve learning. Ironically, the more some teachers try to cram in, the more strategies they employ, the more they squeeze out a key ingredient (arguably, *the* key ingredient) – reflecting on learning.

Maybe reflecting on learning appears too mundane to be significant. Maybe the contrary is true, for when people start talking about metacognition there may be some teachers who dismiss it as yet more jargon, or another bit of theory that bears little resemblance to classroom life.

Yet whatever we call it, *reflecting* on learning – as opposed to *reviewing* information – is hugely significant. And it needn't be dramatic and overly time-consuming. It simply means asking students the questions that will help them dwell on their experiences in a conscious way. If teachers did nothing else but ensure that they consistently asked the questions below as an integral part of the learning process, learning would improve.

- *What have you learned from this?*
- *How did you reach this conclusion?*
- *How did you go about it?*
- *On reflection, was this the best way to approach it?*
- *Would you do the same thing if you were faced with a similar task tomorrow?*
- *How might this experience help you in a similar situation?*
- *What advice would you give to others facing a similar task?*
- *What do you take away from this experience?*

The issue of learning styles is, at root, an equal-opportunities issue.

Paul Ginnis

Two further dimensions

It is also worth highlighting here the importance of two other elements in the learning process:

- choice
- the 're' dimension.

Choice

There is often more than one way to demonstrate understanding. This could involve the teacher providing:

- free choice – *How would you like to show me your understanding?*

- guided choice – *Would you like to show that in a flow-diagram or a cartoon strip? Would you like to draw a labelled diagram or write a short paragraph?*

Providing an element of choice in this stage of the learning process is important for a number of reasons:

1 Giving people a choice puts them in control, and the feeling of being in control is both reassuring and motivating.

2 Providing a choice induces a positive *I want to* decision. (*I want to* draw a cartoon strip.)

3 By giving students a choice, we are allowing them to demonstrate their understanding in a way that makes sense to them, rather than asking them to simply regurgitate information in whatever form it was delivered. This is important because successful learners re-create information rather than simply reproducing it (see page 157).

4 Providing a choice allows the student to play to his or her strengths. At an extreme level, a student may struggle to convey genuine understanding in a piece of writing, but may display an obvious grasp of the same issue in the form of a diagram.

   This issue is best summarised in Howard Gardner's work on multiple intelligences (see *Strategies for Closing the Learning Gap* for more details). Denying students an opportunity to work in their preferred style denies them the opportunity to fully develop and demonstrate their understanding. It is both unfair and immoral.

   For example, when students have the choice of presenting information – or demonstrating their understanding – as either a flow diagram or a cartoon strip, it is likely that students who think and process information in a linear, sequential manner (as opposed to a random, tangential fashion) will choose the flow diagram. Similarly, the gifted musician may choose to convey understanding through a jingle or rap rather than as a piece of prose.

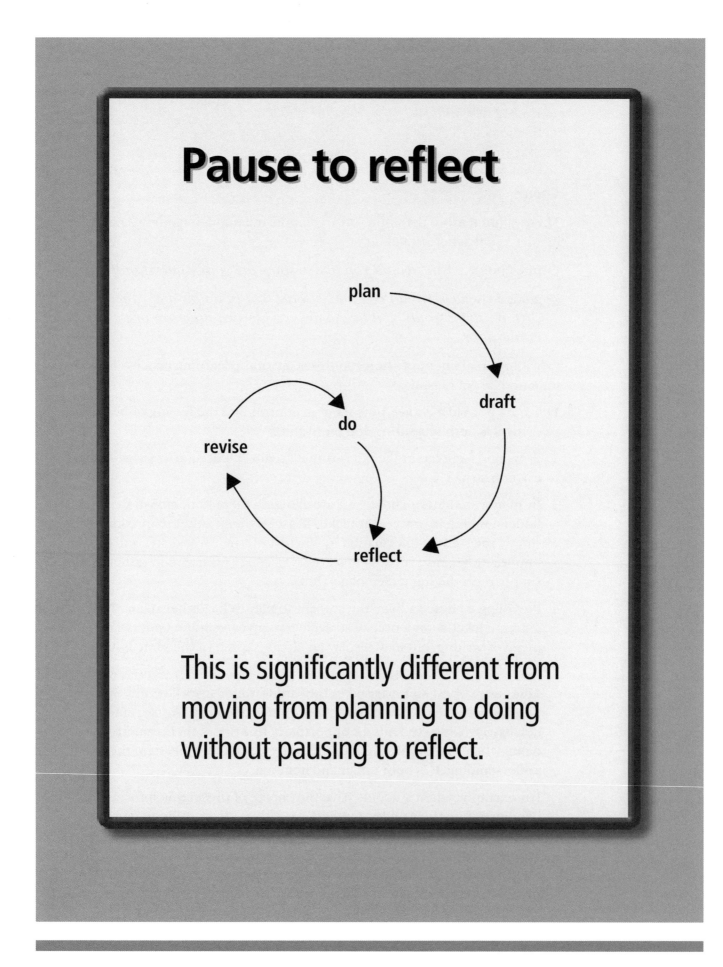

The 're' dimension

Learning does not always happen instantaneously. The penny rarely drops in one go – particularly when the learning is complex and deep. Rather, understanding gradually develops and deepens over time. While knowing has an end-point – you didn't know something but now you do – understanding never stops. This means that there is a significant '*re*' element in deep, meaningful learning.

For example, when learning is taking place students are often:

- re-thinking
- re-assessing
- reforming
- re-drafting
- revisiting
- reconsidering
- revising.

This '*re*' element is prompted by many things, most notably one of three inter-related factors, or a combination of them:

- **Reflection** – when students reflect upon their learning at a conscious level, they may come to the conclusion that their original thinking does not add up.

- **Intervention** – teachers intervene in the learning process in order to mediate the experience (see page 191). This intervention comes in many forms. For example, the teacher might provide additional information that appears to be contradictory to the student's existing explanation of events (see page 125). In order to accommodate the additional information, a re-think is required. Another way in which a teacher might prompt such a re-think is to play devil's advocate.

- **Feedback** – this is a vital ingredient in learning. Feedback comes in many forms and is not confined to formal assessment by the teacher. When a student wires up an electrical circuit, presses the switch and the bulb fails to light up, he is being told that his initial thinking was incomplete, and to try again. When a small child tries in vain to join the like poles of two magnets, she is forced to re-think and try another approach. When a student shows his partner the first draft of a poem, the feedback he receives can inform subsequent amendments.

> **Reflect**
>
> - How much choice do you consciously build into your lessons?
> - If it depends, what does it depend upon?

Indicators of learning

Learning – making meaning – is a bit like the wind; we can't see it, only evidence of it.

Because it is personal and goes on inside the head, it is not always easy to spot. Many things indicate that learning *might* be taking place – but it is not so easy to know for sure. For example, if we glance into a classroom and see children talking to each other it may indicate that learning is taking place – equally, they could be talking about last night's football!

Generating some indicators that learning *might* be taking place is helpful, not least for the discussions that the process will generate. Such a list might include the following:

- **Children are explaining something in their own words.**
- **Children are asking questions.**
- **Children are making connections.**
- **Children are re-creating (rather than reproducing) information.**
- **Children are justifying their decisions.**
- **Children are explaining their thinking.**
- **Children are talking to each other.**
- **Children are active – doing something with information.**
- **Children are reflecting at a conscious level.**
- **Children are offering analogies and metaphors of their own:** *Oh I get it – it's a bit like* ...
- **Children are re-drafting, revising, re-thinking and so on (page 179).**
- **Children are frowning (the penny is stuck) ... and then smiling (as the penny drops).**

Although reflection, intervention and feedback (RIF) take place constantly in the classroom almost by chance, it is more likely that learning will take place when the need to intervene, feed back, prompt reflection and generally encourage students to revisit their thinking is made explicit and consciously planned for.

For example, a learning experience may be planned as follows:

Step 1 Draft out your initial thoughts.

Step 2 Share your ideas with your partner and other students in your group.

Step 3 Reflect upon your first draft in the light of comments made by other people.

During these three steps, the teacher can circulate and intervene when necessary.

Step 4 Revise your initial draft based upon your reflections and the feedback that you have received.

These steps need not take a particularly long time and can be repeated as many times as necessary. The significant point is that teachers are:

- emphasising the importance of revisiting, re-drafting, and so on – as part of the process of learning about learning and becoming better learners, students need to learn the significance of the '*re*' element

- making RIF explicit

- consciously planning for and encouraging students to re-draft and re-think – *plan, reflect, revise, do* is significantly different from moving from planning to doing without pausing to reflect.

How do you know learning is taking place?

This is a question that is very much easier to ask than it is to answer, for while it is relatively easy to know whether or not they *know* something, *learning* is infinitely more difficult to spot. It is hard enough to identify whether learning *has taken place* but at least there are often visible outcomes of learning that provide us with some degree of evidence. Identifying when learning *is taking place* is more challenging again. Yet it is also a key question that teachers and schools must address at a conscious level.

The '*re*' element is a useful indicator, for when students are re-doing and re-thinking they are almost certainly learning, because they are in the process of making sense of new information and the world around them.

Reflect

- How do you know that learning is taking place?
- How does your list of indicators compare with the list opposite?
- To what extent to you build a 're' element into your lessons?

What really distinguishes good teachers from great ones is not so much the way they *teach* (box A), but the extent to which they *help students learn* (box D).

Box D (see page 112)

There is a strong argument that this is the key box. There are a great many teachers who 'do box A' well. They plan interesting lessons, structure them effectively and use appropriate resources. Their classroom and behaviour management skills are well developed, and they explain, instruct and demonstrate with clarity and accuracy. However, there are some teachers who do all that and more and **what really distinguishes good teachers from great ones is not so much the way they teach but the extent to which they help students learn**.

The very fact that we are even considering how teachers help students make sense of information reflects the way that the role of the teacher has evolved in recent years. There was a time when the teacher's job was largely confined to instructing and telling (box A); students either got it or they didn't. Now, while the ability to explain and transfer information remains a prerequisite for effective teaching, the role has expanded and includes helping students develop understanding. Many describe this process as *facilitating learning*.

Facilitating learning is a phrase that is familiar to most if not all teachers, and one that is frequently placed in box D. Yet, despite its widespread usage, it is a relative newcomer to our professional vocabulary, and one wonders if everyone using it knows precisely what it means. Maybe, before we go too much further, it would be helpful to pause and collectively unpick both the language and the concept.

Facilitating learning, or helping people make sense of information and experience, would appear to involve two broad stages:

1 planning

2 responding.

Learning experiences (lessons) are planned in advance. Teachers decide which resources they are going to use, how information is going to be transferred, how the lesson is going to be structured, and so on. This stage can be planned consciously, slowly and collaboratively. Done well, we are increasing the likelihood of learning taking place for, while we cannot guarantee understanding, we are selecting approaches and strategies that make it more likely that students will make sense of the information they encounter.

Yet, put 30 students alone in a room with a high-quality task and it is doubtful if much significant learning will occur. For much depends upon the way in which the teacher orchestrates the process through their questioning, prompting, encouraging, challenging and cajoling. These 'micro' teacher behaviours can be collectively termed *interventions* and play a crucial role in facilitating learning.

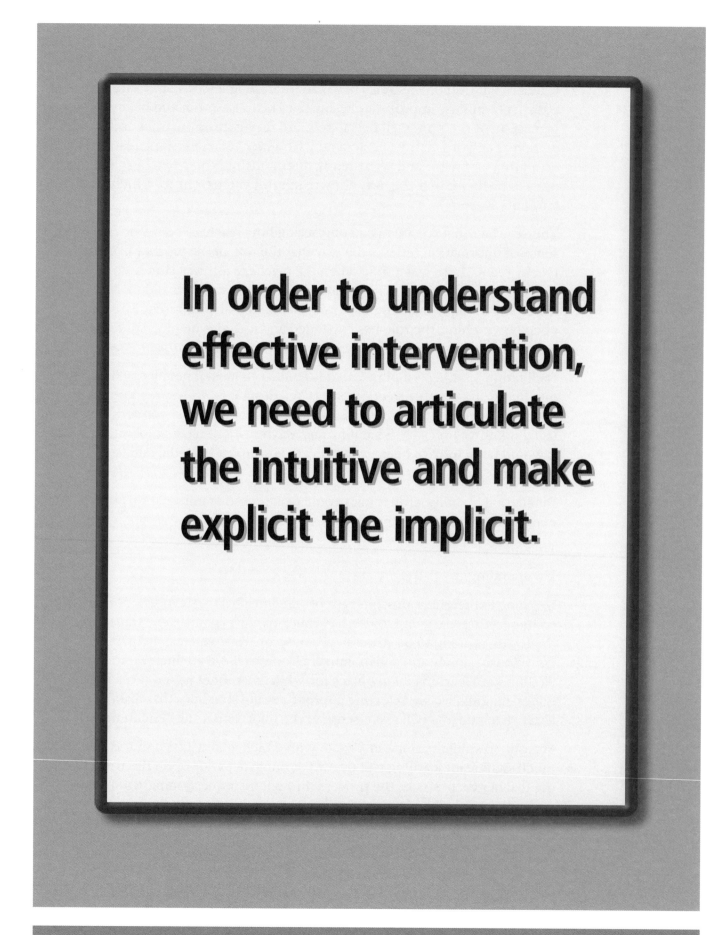

In order to understand effective intervention, we need to articulate the intuitive and make explicit the implicit.

Intervention, then, is a component part of the wider process of facilitation, and lies at the heart of box D. Much intervention is intuitive and instinctive, and often occurs in response to the way in which students respond to the tasks, activities and information they encounter during the lesson. In many respects, then, intervention is a response to a response!

However, while intervention will always retain an instinctive, intuitive element and can never be planned in the same way as a lesson can be, it is possible to consider the whole issue of intervention at a conscious level. **Indeed, it is precisely because effective intervention depends so much upon instinct and intuition that we need to 'unpack' exactly what effective teachers are doing.** A key message of this and other books in the series is that we need to articulate the intuitive and make explicit the implicit.

To recap, consider the following:

- Learning is often enhanced when the process is facilitated by another.

- The intervention of a teacher plays a significant role in helping students make sense of information.

- Some teachers intervene more effectively than others.

- Even the best teachers can improve.

- Although intervention is largely intuitive, it can be considered at a conscious level. While we cannot pre-plan the script, we might be able to generate some useful rules of thumb.

- Many schools have made considerable improvements in the way lessons are planned and structured and in the nature of the tasks that teachers employ. In order to improve further, attention must now turn to the way in which teachers use these tasks and resources in order to facilitate learning.

- This is an area that most certainly needs to be 'unpacked' by teachers themselves. *Telling* teachers how to facilitate learning will have a limited effect; it is an issue that teachers need to reflect upon and talk about, rather than receive training in.

- How teachers facilitate learning and intervene in the learning process could provide a suitable focus for professional development, teacher enquiry and coaching.

Reflect
- How do you respond to the points above?
- What would you wish to add or amend?
- Would learning in your school improve if teachers became more effective at facilitating learning and intervening in the learning process?
- If so, what will be the catalyst for such improvement?

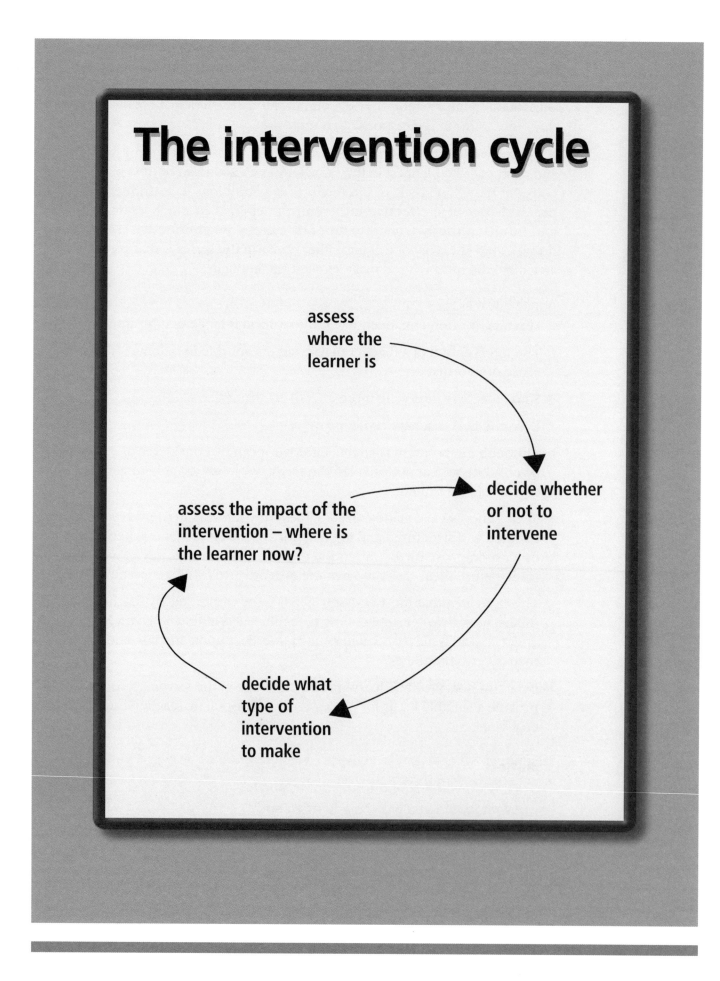

It has been suggested that box D must be unpacked by teachers themselves, to work out what effective intervention looks like in their own context. The following ideas are therefore offered not as ready-made 'answers', but simply as food for thought.

As a starting point, let us remember two things:

- the aim of the exercise – we are seeking to develop and assess *students'* understanding, rather than demonstrate our own
- Reuven Feuerstein's rule of thumb, which is to *Mediate as little as possible but as much as necessary.*

Facilitating learning – helping students 'join the dots'

Teachers cannot give students ready-made meaning – learning involves individuals making meaning for themselves. Here, we make the distinction between giving students the complete picture and helping students join the dots for themselves. The *joining the dots* metaphor is used frequently in this section.

> Helping people join the dots – or make sense of information – would appear to involve four stages:
>
> - **Step 1** – assess where the learner is
> - **Step 2** – decide whether or not to intervene
> - **Step 3** – decide what type of intervention to make
> - **Step 4** – assess the impact of the intervention; where is the learner now?

Having made an intervention – or decided not to – the process of assessing where the leaner is begins again in a constant *assess–decide–act* loop. In reality, as this process often takes place instinctively, the discrete steps merge into one. The intention of this section is to help teachers reflect at a conscious level on something they do intuitively on a daily basis.

Step 1 – assess where the learner is

Three points must be stressed:

1 Teachers cannot assess understanding if the task does not allow students to demonstrate it. Tasks and activities must therefore be designed to allow students to demonstrate their *understanding* rather than prove that they *know*.

2 Teachers must observe and, in particular, listen very carefully to establish a picture of how the student is thinking.

3 If teachers have insufficient evidence to determine where the student currently is, they must seek further information by asking questions, probing, and so on.

To rescue a man lost in the woods, you must first get to where he is.

John Holt, *How Children Fail*

Listening, along with observing, is crucial when establishing where the learner is. Yet listening is one of those things that are often neglected in the classroom. Consider the following. How does a teacher respond when a student with a quizzical look on her face, puts up her hand and says, *I don't get this.*

- **Option A is to talk** - or explain again. This essentially involves transferring the information a second time, possibly using different words or approaching the issue from a different angle. In many respects, this is an attempt to give the student understanding by trying to join the dots for them.

- **Option B is to listen**. By using a prompt such as *Tell me the bit you do know ...,* or *Tell me what you're thinking ...,* or *Do you know what it isn't* ... and then listening to the response, the teacher creates an opportunity to identify any misconceptions, any blockages or gaps in the student's thinking. He is essentially inviting the student to think aloud so that he can establish precisely where she is. Only now is the teacher in a position to decide on the appropriate intervention.

This is not to suggest that teachers should never *tell* students, or transfer information a second and third time. The point that is being made here is that option A and option B are different, and that teachers can easily neglect option B. Interestingly, the best teachers often use both strategies; having listened to the student and identified the blockage, they now provide the necessary additional information. The difference is that, rather than assuming that they know why a student is stuck and therefore what they need to do to help, they take the trouble to find out.

Much has been made in recent years of the need for teachers to provide students with *wait time*, or thinking time, after asking a question. In other words, give students some time to think *before* they give their answer. Much less emphasis has been placed on the need to give some wait time *after* the student has spoken. Many people do not listen when having a conversation – they are simply waiting for their turn to talk, and begin talking immediately after (sometimes before!) the other person has finished speaking.

However, if, after a student has given his answer and finished speaking, the teacher consciously pauses for just a few seconds longer than would be considered normal in everyday conversation, the student is often encouraged to carry on talking. By staying quiet, the teacher is encouraging the student to talk, thereby revealing more and more about the way in which he is thinking about a particular issue.

We are trying to assess where students are and how they are thinking. This means that we need to get to the bottom of their thinking, and one way we can do this is by *listening longer*. By listening longer we are effectively waiting to see if there is anything else we need to know. In a nutshell, **the more we listen, the more they talk - and the more they talk the greater the chance of them revealing the piece of information that we need to ascertain precisely where they are.**

Mediate as little as possible but as much as necessary.

Reuven Feuerstein

Reflect

● Which are you most likely to do first when a student is stuck – talk or listen?

● What do you do when a student finishes talking – talk or remain silent?

● What do you take away from this exercise?

Classrooms are such frenetic places that a few simple rules of thumb can be invaluable to guide teachers' largely instinctive responses. For example, to find out where students are in their understanding:

● listen rather than talk

● listen longer – pause after a student finishes speaking

● say to students, *Tell me what you're thinking.*

Step 2 – to intervene or not to intervene?

To intervene or not to intervene, that is the question. Teachers are constantly making decisions, often at a sub-conscious level, as to whether or not they should intervene in students' learning.

Let our guiding light be Reuven Feuerstein's rule of thumb on the opposite page – *Mediate as little as possible but as much as necessary.*

As a broad generalisation, many teachers often intervene too much and too soon. This early and excessive intervention is often prompted by two major motives:

1 a genuine desire to help – we want students to learn and make progress, and are sometimes uncomfortable when we see them struggling

2 the pressure to move on quickly in order to get through the planned material and cover the syllabus.

Yet sometimes students need to grapple with their learning and be puzzled for a time. Over-intervention, whatever the motive, runs the risk of trying to make sense *for* them and pass on *your* understanding. It may have some short-term benefits, but can easily lead to a sense of dependence among students. Professor Guy Claxton, in his hugely influential *Building Learning Power* programme and book of the same name (see page 252 for details), highlights the fact that effective learners are *resilient*. Indeed, many would argue that persistence is the key attribute of successful people. It is hard to see how students can develop resilience if teachers intervene at the first sign of trouble.

I had to learn how to teach less so that more could be learned.

W. Timothy Gallwey

One possible approach is for teachers to remind students that it is OK to be puzzled. In effect, we are giving them permission to find something difficult. Teachers often tell students that a task is straightforward – if that is true, then students could reasonably expect to complete it without undue trouble. If we consistently tell students that the task is straightforward, then there is a real danger that, at the first sign of difficulty, students come to the conclusion that they can't do something and must therefore be 'thick'.

Maybe there is a need to tell students when a task is tricky. In other words, send a clear message that it is normal to find this hard. When students accept this, we increase the chances that they are prepared to grapple with an issue, and then the only intervention required from the teacher may be the occasional encouraging smile!

Discussing the issue of when to intervene as part of a professional development programme can help raise awareness and encourage teachers to reflect on something that is largely instinctive. Although there can be no hard and fast rules about when a teacher should intervene, as every student and every situation is clearly unique, it may be possible to generate some broad indicators.

If nothing else we might just find teachers pausing for a moment before diving in to 'help', and asking themselves, *Do I really need to intervene at this point?*

Reflect
- When should a teacher intervene?
- Compare your response with those of your colleagues.

Step 3 – decide upon the nature of the intervention

Following on from, and inextricably linked to, the question *Do I need to intervene?* come the questions that help us determine the nature of that intervention. Staying with the 'joining the dots' metaphor, the kind of questions that we might consider are:

- *Do they need more dots?*
- *Is the gap between the dots too large?*
- *Is the gap between the dots too small?*
- *Are the dots in the right place?*

As a broad rule of thumb, it is important to remember that intervention is not about telling students the answer, giving them your understanding and making sense for them. **Intervention is about providing more dots – clues or pointers – that will help unblock their thinking and, when necessary, redirect their attention.**

Intervention is *not* about *telling* students the answer, giving them *your* understanding and making sense *for* them.

Intervention is about providing more dots – clues or pointers – that will help unblock students' thinking and, when necessary, redirect their attention.

Some examples of possible approaches to help unblock students' thinking are suggested below:

- When students are struggling, provide more information – a strategically placed dot or two – that will help clarify their thinking.
- When they need stretching and challenging, provide more information that will *confuse* their thinking. (This is known as cognitive conflict – see page 125.)
- Play devil's advocate.
- Present the same information in a different way. Students that struggle to grasp an oral explanation might well understand when the same information is presented in diagrammatic form.
- Look at the same information from a different angle. For example, students may have trouble understanding the idea of electric current being a flow of charge, but thinking of current in a wire as being like water flowing in a pipe can really help them to 'see' what's happening. This example also illustrates how framing intangible concepts in concrete terms can be very effective in releasing understanding.
- Change the way students are grouped.
- Help students re-word their thinking.
- Give some examples and invite students to add some of their own.
- Model – work through an issue to show students how it is done. The effectiveness of this approach is significantly enhanced when we ask students to describe aloud what we are doing as we demonstrate. It can also be helpful to pose questions to sharpen students' observation: *What did I do first …? What happened when I …?,* and so on. Modelling is not limited to the teacher; other students can be used to demonstrate how something is done: *Watch Louise do that and describe to me what you notice.*
- Help students clarify their thinking: *You said … Can you tell me what you meant by that?*
- Ask students:
  - *What evidence or examples can you give to show me your thinking?*
  - *What further information do you need in order to make sense of this?*
  - *What does a person who understands this know that you don't?*
  - *What question would you want to ask me at this point?*
  - *What would a scientist/artist make of this?*
  - *How do you think a scientist/artist would approach this?*
  - *Tell me what you* **do** *know.*
  - *Can you tell me what the answer* **isn't**? *What can we rule out?*
  - *Give me* **an** *answer (as opposed to* **the** *answer).*
  - *Give me three possible answers – which do you think is the most likely?*
  - *Tell me what you're thinking.*
  - *What would you say if you* **did** *understand?*

When a student responds to an open question, she is doing more than giving an answer.

She is capturing and connecting a swirl of vague, disparate, nebulous thoughts and in the process beginning to complete the unfinished picture that exists in her mind.

Questioning

Facilitating learning and questioning are inextricably linked. However, much depends upon the nature of the questions posed by teachers. For low-level closed questions have more to do with finding out if students know something. These questions have their place but have little to do with facilitating learning. Helping students make sense and deepen their understanding requires questions of an open nature that invite the student to delve deep into their minds and in so doing help them both clarify and reveal their thinking.

When a student responds to such a prompt, she is doing more than answering a question; in effect, she is capturing and connecting a swirl of vague, disparate, nebulous thoughts and in the process beginning to complete the unfinished picture that exists in her mind.

The process of adding to and revealing the picture is not just for the benefit of the teacher; the revelation is also to the benefit of the student. Many writers and researchers tell the story of the student who claims, *I don't know what I'm thinking until I say it.*

If the type of questioning plays such a pivotal role in developing understanding then this is an area that cannot be left to chance and must be considered at a conscious and collective level.

Consider the following:

● There is considerable research that suggests that the most effective teachers ask a higher percentage of open questions than less effective colleagues (see *Effective Teaching* by Muijs and Reynolds – details on page 252).

● The same research suggests that even the most effective teachers ask more low-level closed questions than open ones.

● A great many teachers think they ask more open questions than they actually do.

> **Reflect**
> ● How do you respond to the points above?
> ● What is the balance of open and closed questions in your lessons?
> ● If it depends, what does it depend upon?
> ● Are you basing your answer on what actually happens in your lessons (data) or what you *think* is taking place (perception)?
> ● What do you take away from this exercise?

Helping students 'join the dots'

Step 1 – assess where the learner is

- Listen.
- Listen longer.
- *Tell me what you're thinking.*

Step 2 – decide whether or not to intervene

- Be wary of intervening too much, too soon.
- *Do I really need to intervene at this point?*

Step 3 – decide what intervention to make

- Resist the temptation to provide the answer.
- Provide more dots – clues or pointers – to help unblock or re-direct students' thinking.
- Remember the strategies that make learning more likely: talking, asking questions, reducing, connecting, and so on.

Step 4 – assess the impact of the intervention

- Where is the learner now? Begin the loop again.

Final thoughts on intervention

Bearing in mind that the purpose of intervention is to help people make sense, when we intervene it is helpful to keep firmly in mind the principles established in box C (see page 143) regarding the kinds of activities that make learning more likely. For example, we know that the following help develop understanding, and should therefore be reflected in the nature of our interventions:

- **Talking** helps develop understanding, so as a rule of thumb try to intervene in a manner that enables the learner to talk rather than simply listen.

- **Asking questions** helps people clarify issues – so give students opportunities to pose questions as well as answer them.

- **Doing something** to information demonstrates and develops understanding (see page 153). One of the most useful and versatile strategies is to get people to reduce or prioritise information. For example: *Which do you think is the most significant ... If you had to cut something out, what would you choose ...? Put those three statements in order of importance ...* and so on.

- Understanding is essentially about making **connections**. This can be highlighted and made explicit when intervening in a student's learning. *You've just told me X, and you also know Y and Z. How might those three pieces of information be connected?*

Please note that, although the emphasis in this section has been on how teachers intervene, it should be acknowledged that peers play a significant role in a student's learning.

Step 4 – assess the impact of the intervention

The loop begins again with Step 1, as teachers assess the effectiveness of their intervention by working out where students are *now*.

Reflect
- What form do your interventions in students' learning usually take?
- If it depends, what does it depend upon?
- When students are struggling do you give them the answer or do you help them find it for themselves?

An almost indefinable quality

Sarah is a good teacher. Like so many of the profession, she is doing – given the context – a good job with most of the children, most of the time. One day, Sarah witnessed Tony – an exceptional and highly skilled colleague – calming down Joshua, who was throwing a tantrum. Sarah was incredibly impressed, as Joshua was infamous throughout the school for his regular and fierce tantrum throwing. Indeed, Sarah had first-hand experience of his behaviour – she had tried all she knew to calm the boy when he'd flown off the handle on a previous occasion, but to no avail. As far as she was concerned, Josh was uncontrollable.

Sarah described the incident at the end of the day in tones of awe and wonderment. *You should have seen Tony*, she enthused *He just calmed him down in a matter of seconds.* When she was asked what Tony had done to bring about such a dramatic change in the boy's mood, she replied, *Oh, it was awesome. He just kind of calmed him down. You should have seen it.*

Her questioner was persistent and once again asked her **precisely** what Tony had done. *Oh you should have seen it,* she repeated, It *was fantastic. He just kind of … well, he sort of … well, he just kind of calmed him down.*

The questioner smiled and asked Sarah what she would now do differently if Joshua threw another tantrum. She paused for a moment, sighed as if the significance of the question had just hit home, and replied, *I think I'd go and get Tony!*

Section 5: Case studies – Beyond good

> ❝ *There is an almost indefinable quality that characterises the very best teaching ... You know it when you have seen it but it is hard to define precisely in advance.* ❞

David Bell, then HMCI (from a speech at Gateshead, 27 June 2003)

The challenge for teachers is, and always will be, to develop. For, however well they are doing, there is still an imperative to improve. Yet the focus is changing – the challenge to eradicate poor teaching and ensure competence in our classrooms has largely been met. For the vast majority of schools, the issue now is how to turn *good* and even *very good* lessons into *outstanding* ones. In short, how do we move *beyond good*, from competence to widespread excellence?

David Bell may well be right (above); maybe the very best teaching defies precise definition. Yet the key word in his sentence, and the one that provides us with a glimmer of hope, is 'almost'. It may be difficult to pin it down, but we must try, for if we fail to capture precisely what these outstanding teachers are doing and articulate what the elite often do intuitively, the challenge to improve further on teaching that is already very good will ultimately prove a step too far.

It is worth acknowledging at this point a number of broad generalisations:

- The greater the expertise and the higher the quality of the 'performance', the harder it is to improve. This principle holds true for musicians, chefs, athletes and, of course, teachers.

- Improving from an exceptionally high base involves fine-tuning – paying close attention to small detail. It also involves focusing upon specific aspects or components, rather than on the whole. Great golfers don't set out simply to improve their golf; rather, they work intensively on discrete elements of their game, such as their putting. Similarly, 'improving teaching' is too vague; we need far greater precision.

- Many high fliers, in whatever field, are naturally gifted and instinctive performers. In order to emulate their success we must articulate the intuitive, make explicit the implicit and convert what comes naturally to them into conscious practice and concrete strategies.

A central message of this book has been that improvements from such a high base demand an approach rooted in learning – reflection, enquiry and coaching – rather than simply monitoring and telling teachers what to do next. In this spirit, therefore, the following pages are offered not offered as stock answers, but rather as ideas and starting points to stimulate thought and discussion.

Few would disagree that good teachers engage students in their learning. If this is true, what do great teachers do?

Playing on the alliteration, one might tentatively suggest that *great* teachers:

- **entice**
- **enthral**
- **excite**.

Beyond engagement

Reflect

Is moving from *good* to *great* about:
- doing the same things better, or more often?
- doing things differently?
- doing the same things *and* adding a bit more?

Few would disagree that good teachers engage students in their learning. If this is true, what do great teachers do?

Playing on the alliteration, one might tentatively suggest that *great* teachers:

- **entice**
- **enthral**
- **excite**.

If that is accepted – and clearly some teachers have the ability to enthral and excite students – then the question that we must address is *how* do they do that? We are not seeking a single, secret recipe, for there is rarely a one-size-fits-all answer; rather, we want to identify some discrete ingredients that we can adapt and adopt in our own practice.

Working backwards, would *you* be enthralled and excited if:

- there was no sense of challenge?
- everything made perfect and immediate sense to you?

If the answer to these prompts is *no*, then we have some pointers as to what great teachers are doing in the classroom.

For it would appear that people are enthralled and excited when:

- there is a sense of **challenge**
- they are **curious** …
- … and people become curious, not to mention challenged, when things do not add up immediately – in other words, when they are puzzled or **confused**.

A strong theme running throughout this book is that learning involves *constructing* meaning and *making* sense, and that while good teachers provide students with the completed picture, **great teachers help students join the dots themselves**.

Which best describes your classroom?

I generate a sense of interest.	I generate a sense of curiosity.
I engage students.	I entice and excite students.
I go out of my way to clarify and make things simple.	I go out of my way to create a sense of confusion.
I give students the complete picture.	I help students join the dots.
We review information.	We reflect on learning.

Let us break down what good teachers and great teachers are doing in their lessons, into specific behaviours.

Good teachers:

- transfer information concisely and accurately
  - ▶ in easily digestible chunks
  - ▶ in a variety of ways
  - ▶ in a way that is easy to understand
- generate a sense of interest
- engage students in activity
- review information
- provide pictures …

Great teachers do all this *and more*. They excite, enthral and entice, by:

- challenging students
- generating a sense of curiosity
- deliberately providing a puzzle and creating a sense of confusion …

They optimise learning by:

- recognising that students need to talk about their learning and verbalise their thinking
- encouraging students to explore and extend their thinking by posing their own questions
- including a strong sense of reflection in their lessons
- helping students join the dots themselves.

The above points are not in any sense presented as a definitive list, rather as:

1 a catalyst for discussion – if great teachers *don't* do the above, what *do* they do?

2 a possible focus for enquiry – if we accept that great teachers manage to generate a sense of curiosity in students, then the question that we need to address is, *how do they do that?*

Reflect

- How do you respond to the bullet points above?
- What would you wish to add or amend?

The rest of this section is devoted to four small case studies – examples of enquiry, practice and developments that have taken place in real schools. They are not presented here as models of excellence, simply to stimulate debate and reflection.

It is, in fact, nothing short of a miracle that the modern methods of instruction have not entirely strangled the holy curiosity of enquiry.

Albert Einstein

Example: Farlingaye High School, Suffolk – *focus on curiosity*

Sarah Bainton, Deputy Headteacher

Background

- 11–18 comprehensive, Specialist School Status – Maths and Computing

- NOR 1632

- Leading Edge School, Ambassador School Status

- Semi-rural location

Context

Examination results have been improving steadily over a number of years, culminating in a 5 A*–C rate of 69% in 2005. In the same year, the overall points score at A level of 397 was the highest in Suffolk.

The OFSTED inspection of 2002 concluded that the school was outstanding, with no key areas to address and no teaching that was unsatisfactory. With such success, it might have been tempting for teachers to have 'rested on their laurels' and felt that there was no need for further improvement. This, however, was not the case and there remains a desire to go on developing in order to raise standards still further.

Teaching and learning

The school adopted the four-phase lesson advocated by Mike Hughes as a template for lesson design. Staff training took place through in-house CPD sessions and PD days with particular emphasis on the 'making sense' dimension. All departments looked at schemes of work, and considered where appropriate learning strategies could be introduced in their teaching.

Teaching and Learning Group

The work on teaching and learning continued to build and eventually led to the formation of a Teaching and Learning Group. This group is made up of interested volunteers with every curriculum area being represented. It meets every three weeks to explore areas related to teaching and learning.

Curiosity

Our focus of attention during 2005–06 has been curiosity – how we generate it in students, and how we recognise it when we see it. This whole area has generated some fantastic discussions and has encouraged us to try out a range of new ideas in our teaching. As fascinating as it was, we all found that 'curiosity' is extremely difficult to pin down. We also felt that it is something that must be explored and experienced rather than read about. The summary of our experiences on the next few pages are offered as food for thought in the hope that they may spark off some discussion, reflection and experimentation in the classroom.

Curiosity – the key ingredients

- **novelty**
- **surprise**
- **puzzle**
- **challenge**
- **mystery**
- **prediction**
- **confusion**

Reflect

1 How do you respond to the above list?

2 What would you wish to add to it?

3 To what extent are these ingredients present in your lessons?

Step 1

We began by asking ourselves the questions:

1 *How do we make students curious?*

2 *What does curiosity look like?*

At the end of a most fascinating discussion, we agreed to look closely at these issues in our lessons and keep a note of strategies that seemed to be effective.

At our second meeting, we generated the following questions for discussion:

- *What is curiosity?*
- *How do we know students are curious – what are the signs of curiosity?*
- *Can curiosity manifest itself in different ways?*
- *Does curiosity mean change?*
- *Does curiosity always lead to engagement?*
- *Can you get engagement first, which then leads to curiosity?*
- *Is curiosity subject to certain conditions? Do teachers have to create the right conditions before students will become curious?*
- *Does good questioning always lead to curiosity?*

Step 2

We all spent the next three weeks focusing on curiosity to see if we could answer some of the questions that had been raised. This was quite a challenge!

Inevitably, our attention turned to strategies and approaches that we could use as teachers in order to generate a sense of curiosity in our students. For many of us, this involved trying out new ideas in our classroom.

A number of interesting issues began to emerge and we began to:

- discuss whether curiosity and engagement were the same, and how the two could be distinguished
- look closely at the language used to generate interest and curiosity
- explore whether curiosity could be sustained in and between lessons
- distinguish between curiosity generated as a result of a conscious strategy and what we termed *happy accidents*
- explore the extent to which teachers could deaden natural curiosity
- wonder if students sometimes hid their curiosity – is there a *it's not cool to be curious* culture in some teenagers?

Step 3

We continued to gather activities and experiences where we felt we had made students curious. Not surprisingly, the precise implementation of these strategies had a strong subject-specific dimension. However, we began to list some generic strategies that all teachers could adapt and then employ in their lessons. These can be found on the following pages.

Work it out

The teacher opens the classroom door and beckons the first four children into the room, indicating that the others should remain.

A few minutes later – the children in the corridor are already whispering furiously, wondering what is going on – the teacher allows the rest of the class through the door.

They enter the classroom to find four children slumped over the front desks. One of them is wearing a Homer Simpson mask (from the popular TV show). On the board is written *What happened to Simpson?*

The explanation – if you're curious – can be found on page 215.

Thanks to Jan Molyneux, Marlborough School Science College, for sharing this highly unusual lesson start.

Some ideas for generating a sense of curiosity

1 Do something different with the classroom. Change the room layout or orientation, or the wall displays. Play music as students enter the classroom. Turn the desks upside down – for a lesson on WWI, one teacher upturned desks to create the trenches.

2 The teacher does something unusual – wear a gas mask or a costume, talk in German (see **3**) or use sign language (see **15**).

3 Use open-ended questions to frame the lesson. For example, as students entered the room their History teacher welcomed them with a smile and *Guten tag*. The students were clearly surprised and enquired if the teacher was OK! *I'm just wondering,* replied the teacher, *do you think we'd all be talking in German today if Hitler had invaded immediately after Dunkirk?* Questioning was found to be an effective way of stimulating thinking and curiosity. One rule of thumb was to take the well-known Bloom's Taxonomy and make a conscious effort to begin the lesson with higher level questions.

4 Anything unexpected is likely to spark interest and curiosity. For example, one lesson involved a series of photographs, diagrams, and so on, that were turned upside-down so that the students couldn't see them. The teacher then described each image – *When you turn over, you will see a picture of a nurse.* When the students turned over the photograph, they did see a nurse – a black, male nurse. It was a great way of confronting stereotypes. Another example was a map of the world – when it was turned over it revealed a Pacific-centric world map – again, not what they were expecting.

5 Prediction is a good way to stimulate curiosity because it requires students to speculate. There are many variations around this theme – *What happened next? What will happen when ...? What would have happened if ...?* and so on.

6 Linked to prediction is imagination. *Imagine a world without the telephone* or *... without gravity. Imagine what would have happened if Humpty hadn't fallen off the wall – would he still be there? Imagine what the world would be like if people could breath under water.* During one of these 'imagine' lessons, one boy posed the question, *Imagine a world with no imagination.* One phrase that is particularly evocative and powerful is *I wonder ...*

7 Mysteries and puzzles are highly effective at drawing students in. For example, as students were about to enter the classroom the teacher, wearing rubber gloves and a white coat, stopped them at the door brandishing a notice which read CRIME SCENE – DO NOT DISTURB EVIDENCE. On the floor was the outline of a murder victim and on the board was written, *Who committed the murder? How? What was the motive?* and so on. Aside from the Colonel Mustard jokes, this was a highly effective way of beginning a lesson.

8 A puzzle is anything that doesn't make immediate sense. An effective way of starting a lesson can be to give students seemingly contradictory information. For example:

There is ice on Mars. There is no water on Mars.

We are now moving into the realm of **cognitive conflict** and it is clear that confusion and curiosity are inextricably linked (see page 221).

9 An easy way to get students curious is to start the lesson with an unidentified artefact or picture. Pictures taken from unusual angles have the same effect. One variation is to sit in silence until students begin to speculate as to what it is. An alternative is to pose a series of questions: *What is it? Where does it come from? What year was it made?* and so on. This can be linked to a *Yes/No* game – the students can ask the teacher questions about it but the replies can only be *yes* or *no.* Another variation is to provide two or more unidentified artefacts and to challenge students to work out how they are linked.

Sentences to get them thinking at the start of a lesson

- Would wrapping a snowman in a coat make it melt more slowly or more quickly?

- How are lungs like Hogwarts?

- What is the connection between a mosquito and a penguin?

- What if there was no friction – would we all travel faster or would we fly?

- Would a cup of tea cool more quickly with cold milk in or without?

- What if …

    … there was double the amount of oxygen in the atmosphere?

    … solids did not dissolve in water?

    … the Earth stopped orbiting the Sun and stayed in one place?

    … there was no wind?

- Why does the sea level not go down as we extract more oil from the North Sea?

- Why does a fly stick to a spider's web but a spider does not?

- Think of 5 similarities and 5 differences between sand and sandpaper.

- What is the connection between a daisy and a worm?

Andy Love, Science AST, Waingels College, Reading

10 A variation on the 'unidentified artefact' theme involves an object, picture or diagram that is at first hidden from view. The artefact is then revealed a piece at a time (a bit like the game on the well-known TV program *Catchphrase)*.

11 A further variation is to allow the students to handle an artefact when blindfolded, or when the object is hidden inside a sack or box.

12 The *Yes/No* game can be used in many ways – a really simple way to start a lesson is to ask the students, *What am I thinking?* They are allowed to pose questions which will be answered *yes* or *no*.

13 One approach that can work well in practical subjects is to lay out all of the tools, equipment and resources before the lesson. As the students enter the room, they have to work out what the lesson is about and what they are going to be doing.

14 Similarly, start the lesson by immediately launching into an activity without explaining why, what the learning objectives are, and so on. Pause after a while and see if the students can work out the learning objectives from the activity. Any change in the normal lesson routine or structure is novel and will raise the odd eye-brow.

15 Keep them guessing at the start of the lesson by not talking. Instead, adopt the 'air hostess' routine and just point, gesticulate and generally demonstrate in silence. This works well when the teacher is demonstrating a new skill or technique as the students have to watch particularly closely. For example, a teacher demonstrated the technique of mono printing in silence and as she did so students began to talk, asking, *What are you doing? Are we going to do this? Are you going to put this on there? Try it this way Miss … Oh I get it!*

16 As students enter the room a quotation is waiting for them on the board. For example:

Great God! This is an awful place.

The students have to work out who said it, when it was said, what it refers to, and so on. This strategy can also be linked to the *Yes/No* game. (The answers with regard to this quotation are on page 215.)

17 Strategies to stimulate curiosity need not be elaborate or take an enormous amount of time to prepare – we are simply making a conscious effort to grab students' attention. Try speaking very quietly to one student or a small group and observe the effect on the rest of the group.

18 One of the most widespread and effective strategies we used involved sealed envelopes. Anything can go into the envelopes – information, instructions, character details, timelines, and so on. There are many variations around the theme. For example, give each group of students an envelope containing something different. At first, do not allow students to see what is in the other groups' envelopes. This can be linked with the 'assemble information' strategy outlined on page 159 – one by one, each group reveals to the class what is in their envelope, and students try to work out how the items might be connected, or assembled together to create something meaningful.

Arguably, the strategy that generated most curiosity – students could hardly contain themselves – was simply to place a sealed envelope on the desk and say something like, *The stuff in this envelope is absolute dynamite – but I'm not going to let you open it yet. Please don't start thinking about what might be in it.*

The Curiosity Indicator

Issue a group of students with a pro forma such as the one below.

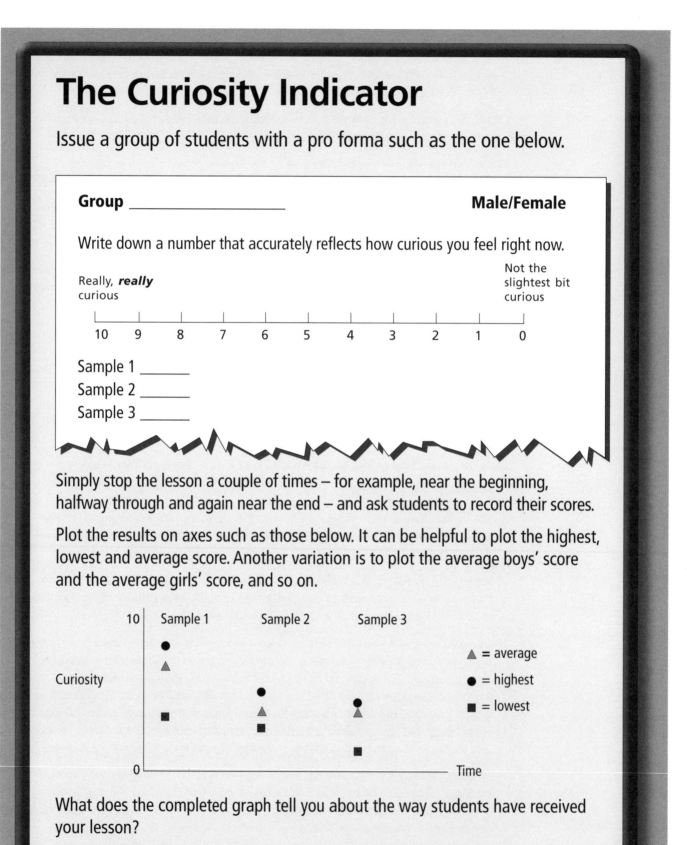

Group _____   **Male/Female**

Write down a number that accurately reflects how curious you feel right now.

Really, *really*
curious

Not the
slightest bit
curious

10	9	8	7	6	5	4	3	2	1	0

Sample 1 _____
Sample 2 _____
Sample 3 _____

Simply stop the lesson a couple of times – for example, near the beginning, halfway through and again near the end – and ask students to record their scores.

Plot the results on axes such as those below. It can be helpful to plot the highest, lowest and average score. Another variation is to plot the average boys' score and the average girls' score, and so on.

Curiosity

10 — Sample 1   Sample 2   Sample 3

▲ = average
● = highest
■ = lowest

0 ——————————————————————— Time

What does the completed graph tell you about the way students have received your lesson?

For general information about using tools such as this, see page 38.

19 A Y11 class studying Shakespeare entered a classroom to find a slideshow of images projected onto a screen. There was no discussion or instruction as to what to do. The students watched – in silence at first, but they gradually began to talk … *That must be from the bit where … That's not how I see that character … I wonder why those images are in the 'wrong' order?*

20 Read the opening sentence or paragraph of a story. Provide a number of possible concluding sentences. Students have to predict which is the correct one.

For example, the opening sentence from a book is:

- *It was a bright cold day in April and the clocks were striking thirteen.*

Which of these is the correct ending to the book?

- *It really was an April to remember.*

- *Although I now lived in the future, I would never forget the time when I lived in the past.*

- *But it was alright, everything was alright, the struggle was finished. He had won the victory over himself. He loved Big Brother.*

- *As the last chimes died away the Gnomish King vanished among the glistening trees.*

- *Though I was now safe, I knew that I would never rid myself of the chilling thought that somebody, somewhere would be hearing a clock strike thirteen.*

Now read a short extract from the middle of the book and give students the chance to revise their first choice of ending if they want to.

For example:

- *The past was erased, the erasure was forgotten, the lie became the truth.*

The answer is given below.

21 There is an old adage: *Never end a lesson with a full stop, always a question mark.* It is a useful rule of thumb. Where possible try to leave students with a puzzle or mystery – something to keep them guessing before the next lesson.

Answers – for those whose curiosity has the better of them!

The explanation of the 'Work it out' scenario on page 210 is that it was Simpson who first discovered an effective and usable anaesthetic. The scene depicts him and his colleagues after their experimentation with chloroform!

The quotation used in example **16** on page 213 was from Captain Robert Falcon Scott, on arriving at the South Pole on 18 January 1912, to find that he had been beaten there by Amundsen.

In example **20** above, the opening and middle sentences are from *1984* by George Orwell, and the correct final sentence is *But it was alright, everything was alright, the struggle was finished. He had won the victory over himself. He loved Big Brother.'*

We started out looking at what makes students curious – but one of the best outcomes was 17 curious teachers!

Teacher, Farlingaye High School

Outcomes

Focusing attention on such a specific aspect of teaching has undoubtedly:

- forced us to think very carefully about what we do
- stimulated a huge amount of interest, discussion and debate
- encouraged all of us to experiment and try out new strategies
- provided a vehicle for sharing ideas and strategies
- improved our teaching
- been enjoyable!

Students have generally responded very positively indeed. One thing became increasingly apparent: even when we failed to generate genuine and deep-rooted curiosity, we invariably managed to get students engaged and interested – and many teachers would settle for that!

Among the comments made by teachers when evaluating the impact of our work, were:

- *Sharing ideas like this has helped each teacher add to their personal 'toolbox'.*
- *I have found the topic of curiosity intellectually stimulating and have very much enjoyed engaging with colleagues.*
- *This has helped remind me why I'm doing this job and who it is for – the kids.*
- *It has made me feel better about myself – I know I care and it's nice to know that others do to.*
- *Better lessons have led to fewer classroom management issues.*
- *I have found that the experience has encouraged me to develop my questioning within the classroom.*
- *Simply talking about what works is really useful.*
- *If you don't get to real learning curiosity, then at least you get interaction and engagement – and that's nothing to be unhappy about.*
- *The issue of curiosity has made me raise the level of challenge, taking students out of their comfort zone – and me out of mine.*
- *It has reminded me that a confused face is a good face – as long as it is followed by a 'light bulb moment'.*
- *We started out looking at what makes students curious – but one of the best outcomes was 17 curious teachers!*

The cure for boredom is curiosity. There is no cure for curiosity.

Ellen Parr

Example: Ash Green School, Warwickshire – *Curiosity Month*

Graham Tyrer, Headteacher

Context:

● 11–16 mixed comprehensive

● NOR 652

Background

Like so many schools, we have been taking steps to improve learning in the classroom. We recognise that this requires significantly more than a one-off Inset day, and consequently embarked on a longer-term journey working alongside Mike Hughes who has acted as our critical friend, mentor and guide.

We seek more than competence. We aspire to be a school in which children are more than engaged – enthralled by the possibilities of the world. We want students to think divergently, to ask questions, to enquire together, to be responsible for the leadership of their learning. That's our vision.

Above all, we want students to feel the richness of learning, its possibilities and to join with us in making lessons ever more exciting. Or, as one of our staff put it, *Let's get back the sheer pleasure of learning itself.*

What we did

If you want something to happen, you have to make a commitment to it. To that end, we devoted an Inset day to exploring the kind of energy that we needed in our lessons to move them from satisfactory to outstanding, from engaging pupils to enticing them, from occupying them to captivating them.

Mike led the session and began by posing the questions, *What makes you curious? Think of times when you have been curious. What makes you wonder? Think of times when you've been caught by an idea, a problem just out of reach.* And we were off! Staff talked and talked about lessons and ideas that had made students think and wonder, doubt and question. We realised we were on to something – curiosity!

We came up with the idea of planning and teaching *Super-lessons* in a *Curiosity Month.*

● The rest of the day was devoted to staff working in their Subject Teams, to plan *the best lesson ever!* – one-off lessons that would really get the students curious and excited. Part of the thinking was that very few individuals are outstanding at everything but by planning in teams the teacher who is a whiz with ICT could work alongside the teacher who has particularly imaginative ideas for starting lessons, the teacher who excels at accommodating kinaesthetic learners, and so on. One notable feature was the way in which staff challenged themselves and others, rejecting ideas that were merely good and largely orthodox in search of activities and approaches that would elevate the lesson into the realms of novel and outstanding.

- June 2006 was designated *Curiosity Month*. Students in Years 8 and 9 were informed that they would see staff working with each other to really get this energy of curiosity going in their classrooms.

- The Super-lesson plans were published and distributed to all staff. Teachers were told that if any lessons made them curious we would arrange, by mutual agreement, for them to be able to observe. Not all staff wanted to see each other work but plenty did. We even commissioned a local media collective to make a DVD of lessons where staff felt particularly excited by what they were doing.

Examples

- Modern linguists invented whole new languages because they were curious about what made language rules.

- Geographers wondered, with students, why the moon was the shape, colour and texture it was – they worked with the Science Team on molecular structure and light wavelengths.

- English staff worked with students, wondering what made world-class literature so celebrated.

- PHSE staff made students curious about leadership and how to redefine it.

- Musicians wondered whether they could interpret History on the flute!

Outcomes

Curiosity Month was a fascinating and energising experience that generated much discussion and reflection. More than that, it provided a vehicle for increased collaboration and peer observation, and generated loads of new ideas for lessons. Not surprisingly, these ideas were not confined to Curiosity Month and began to infiltrate 'ordinary' lessons.

Let the last word go to a member of staff:

 This has revived my faith in what I'm doing. It's not just about jumping through hoops.

Teacher, Ash Green School

... we tried to unpick the question:
What is the difference between good and great learning and teaching?

Our on-going work with Mike Hughes led us to the hypothesis that maybe the difference between good and great is that rather than always giving students all the pieces and the complete picture, a great teacher leaves out or holds back some pieces, adds one or two pieces from a different puzzle, creates a sense of curiosity in learners and then supports them in completing the puzzle for themselves.

Karl Sampson, Deputy Headteacher, saltash.net community school

Example: saltash.net community school, Cornwall – *focus on confusion (cognitive conflict)*

Karl Sampson, Deputy Headteacher

Background

● 11–18 mixed comprehensive school in south-east Cornwall

● NOR 1354

● combined specialism in Science, Mathematics and Computing with a Rural Dimension

Focus on learning

The school works extremely closely to develop learning with its seven primary partner schools and there is a lot of collaborative work taking place in this area. As has already been stated, our mantra comes from Stephen Covey – *The main thing, is to keep the main thing, the main thing* – and for us the main thing is **learning**.

A forum for sharing practice

Over the last two years, a Learning and Teaching Group has been established. The group meets once per half term, is cross phase and attendance is voluntary. There are regularly 20 to 30 staff demonstrating, discussing and exploring learning through sharing practice and other stimulus material. The group is having a real impact on the learning of both students and staff in the different Saltash schools and has become a significant forum for developing learning and teaching.

The first year was dedicated to showcasing effective practice and how each example could be adapted across the phases. However, it was felt that as we moved into year 2 we should take a theme and really begin to 'drill down' and examine the deeper implications for learning.

The changes to school inspection with a focus on self-evaluation and the role of the teacher in terms of 'what they are doing to enable effective learning to take place' seemed to be a natural starting point. When combined with the knowledge that 68% of lessons observed by OFSTED are now judged to be good, we tried to unpick the question: ***What is the difference between good and great (outstanding) learning and teaching?***

Our on-going work with Mike Hughes led us to the hypothesis that maybe the difference between *good* and *great* is that rather than always giving students all the pieces and the complete picture, a great teacher leaves out or holds back some pieces, adds one or two pieces from a different puzzle, creates a sense of curiosity in learners and then supports them in completing the puzzle for themselves.

Creating confusion

Having done some previous work on thinking skills we decided to concentrate on the idea of great or outstanding teachers being able to deliberately create a degree of confusion for their students. In thinking skills programmes, this is referred to as *cognitive conflict* and as a concept was known to many of the group. Indeed, the phrase would be recognised by any teacher who has experience of CASE, CAME or CATE (Cognitive Acceleration through Science/Maths/Design and Technology Education) or is familiar with the work of people like David Leat and Peter Fisher and publications such as *Thinking through Geography* and *Thinking through History*. (See page 253 for details.)

A thinking skills approach – in everyday words:

1 Remind students what they know – touch base

2 Throw a spanner in the works – puzzle them a bit

3 Let them work it out together – support when necessary

4 Talk about how they went about it

5 Think about how this might help them in other situations

However, there is possibly a danger that many teachers:

- see cognitive conflict as something that is confined to thinking skills lessons – there are many stories of students saying things like, *Oh is this one of those lessons when we're supposed to think?*

- are put off by what they regard as jargon and theory.

Our aim therefore was to:

- use the principles that underpin classic thinking skills lessons, such as cognitive conflict, in 'everyday' lessons

- de-mystify the terminology.

De-mystifying

Many thinking skills programmes are built around five key principles or stages:

1 concrete preparation

2 cognitive conflict

3 social construction

4 metacognition

5 transfer and bridging.

The language alone is enough to deter many people! There is a real danger that some teachers will see this as something else they 'have to do', and yet another initiative to add to their workload. Yet when these principles are translated into everyday language, they do not seem anywhere near as daunting:

1 Remind students what they know – touch base.

2 Throw a spanner in the works – puzzle them a bit.

3 Let them work it out together – support when necessary.

4 Talk about how they went about it.

5 Think about how this might help them in other situations.

Use of analogy

The analogy which we used as a group was setting learners off on an apparently straightforward task and then '*throwing a spanner in the works*'. (An extract from our learning@saltash.net newsletter can be found on the next page.)

We also liked the analogy of *gum* and *chewing* as identified by Michael Doyle and David Straus. In the classroom, the *gum* is the content (task) that the teacher uses. The *chewing* is the processing time and strategies that the teacher provides, allowing the students to reflect, hear others, state and share their thoughts and opinions as well as being able to generate and test their ideas.

Extract from learning@saltash.net newsletter

Cognitive conflict is a term that describes a way of teaching students to think. It happens when a natural line of reasoning gets interrupted by something unexpected, forcing you to re-organise your thinking altogether. You set someone off on a problem, they get it sorted and then you 'throw a spanner in the works'. It's part of a strategy known as 'cognitive acceleration'. You have to create learning activities that foster the mental anguish of working things out in group discussion. The most effective teachers, old and new, are excellent at creating 'mental anguish'. They use the classic 'tricks up the teacher's sleeve' to lead students up the garden path and then, suddenly, make them question their assumptions!

Experiences

During the meetings this year, we have begun to explore these ideas and, as a group, trial some cognitive conflict activities with our classes and with each other. We have then discussed their implications for learning across the different phases. The results so far have been really interesting for all sorts of reasons.

- We have picked up lots of great ideas to trial in our classrooms.

- There has been much fun and laughter when trialling the activities at the group meetings.

- Staff are much less reluctant to come and share their ideas.

- Collaborative learning has been really motivating and invigorating for staff, especially at the end of a hard day.

- The level of discussion and dialogue that follows each meeting has been instrumental in moving our thinking forward.

- The value of a cross-phase group has been highlighted as we are now able to engage in dialogue about approaches to cognitive conflict being used from reception classes right through to year 13.

- We have just begun a cross-phase project for KS2 and KS3 teachers which focuses on cognitive conflict in mathematics.

- There has been an increase in use of these strategies in the classroom, as evidenced by lesson observation and the use of ICT technical staff time to help teachers make full use of the interactive whiteboards.

- Feedback from students has been very positive – they are already commenting on how the increased use of these strategies is challenging their thinking as well as making their learning more interesting and more motivating.

Three things became increasingly apparent and are worth highlighting here.

1 Getting the level of confusion right is important. If students are totally bewildered and cannot begin to make sense of the situation they tend to give up mentally. Throwing the right size spanner into the works is a key challenge for teachers.

2 Confusing students is not sufficient for a meaningful learning experience. The way in which the teacher supports and guides students through the process is critical. This involves questioning, providing feedback, playing devil's advocate, and so on. Without this support there is a danger that the experience can become meaningless as some students simply lapse into wild guessing and explain away the confusion with clearly irrational statements.

3 Focusing exclusively on cognitive conflict can be a little narrow. There are obvious links between creating confusion and generating curiosity in students. Many of the things we were looking to develop in the classroom conveniently begin with the letter C:

▶ Confusion

▶ Curiosity

▶ Challenge

▶ Creativity

And it became increasingly clear that they are all inextricably linked.

The provision of cognitive conflict is also a characteristic of much teaching that would be considered 'good' by expert observers.

Philip Adey and Michael Shayer,
Really Raising Standards

Examples

We spent time at our meetings looking at, and actually participating in, activities that had been used by members of the group during lessons. Some of these had been devised from scratch while others had been adapted from existing resources and thinking skills programmes such as CAME.

One of the intentions was to help teachers see how the principles that underpinned a particular activity could be adapted for their particular subject and age-range. Not surprisingly, as we got to grips with the activities, our understanding of how these types of strategies would work in our own classrooms, and our confidence to adapt and adopt them, grew.

Cognitive conflict in History using 'Mysteries'

This meeting focused on a thinking skills strategy known as 'Mysteries'. The basic premise is simple: you give the students a problem or 'mystery' that needs a solution and provide them with pieces of evidence that they need to classify, discuss and possibly discard in order to complete the task. However, the evidence is not quite as straightforward as it seems with a couple of red herrings and more than one solution appearing to be valid. The key is using carefully thought-out questions and prompts in order to generate lots of discussion, reasoning and argument amongst the groups of students. The Learning Group was faced with a 'mystery' focusing on a pit disaster in the 19th Century and who was responsible for it.

The teachers' thinking was physically evident as they moved around the table-top the slips of paper on which evidence about the disaster was supplied. That way, they were able to change their minds as they shared their thinking – the moving actually helped them to think. It was possible to see the progression in their thinking in the way the data items were grouped and structured and by listening to the teachers talking.

Creativity in Design and Technology

The meeting was led by one of our Advanced Skills Teachers (ASTs), and focused on creativity and thinking skills in product design. It was an absolutely fascinating session in which he encouraged the group to think differently and apply their creative talents to the full.

The first task involved being given a picture of part of a domestic appliance, a pencil and some colours which could then be used to complete the picture. The results were staggering, with some people completing the original picture and others turning it into something completely different. It was really interesting to see other people's work and explore the thoughts behind it.

The second task was also extremely interesting as we were given established designers or artists and then asked to take their 'trademark' design styles and apply them to a completely different product. For example:

Imagine if ... Bridget Riley designed dresses

Imagine if ... Alessi designed clothes

Imagine if ... Bertie Bassett designed cars

Imagine if ... Picasso designed ties

Many of the things that move lessons from **good** to **great** conveniently begin with the letter **C**:

- **confusion**
- **curiosity**
- **challenge**
- **creativity**

Cognitive conflict in Mathematics using CAME

The meeting was presented by our other AST, who led an extremely thought-provoking session on 'Thinking skills in Mathematics' using some of the CAME material (*Cognitive Acceleration through Maths Education*, see page 253). The central problem was how to find the best size desk for you. We began by looking at pictures of a variety of desks and picking out and discussing as a pair, and then as a whole group, the characteristics of a good desk – not the kind of thing you would expect to do in a maths lesson! We then discussed terms such as height, width and length and were given equipment to measure ourselves in any way we wished, to generate some basic measurements for our ideal desk – cue much hilarity! We then got into groups to share our findings and collate them in a table. This led into discussions about different types of average, and range, as we had to consider the ideal size desk for our little group, then for a Year 7 class and then to meet the needs of all students in the school.

Cognitive conflict using Visual Literacy

This session was led by one of our LEA Teaching and Learning consultants and focused on the skills associated with reading images, to help develop thinking skills associated with:

- creativity – for example, making hypotheses, and applying imagination

- information processing – for example, analysing part–whole relationships

- reasoning – for example, giving reasons for opinions, making inferences and deductions.

Participants were greeted with a looping ICT presentation of a series of WWI recruitment posters, with a question next to each one (nothing earth shattering here). However, the question did not match with the adjacent poster – it related to the next one in the sequence. It was a highly effective starter activity, which immediately aroused curiosity and ensured that the participants really studied the images to try to comprehend the questions, which were at variance with the posters. It was just like the classic Two Ronnies 'Mastermind' sketch in which Ronnie Corbett's specialist subject was answering the previous question.

We then went on to look at a number of different techniques for reading images, maximising the use of the interactive whiteboard to do this effectively. Strategies we looked at included:

- the five 'W's – *Why? When? What? Where? Who?*

- annotation – to highlight symbolism and decipher images

- living images – the use of empathetic questions around an image to help scaffold student thinking

- squares – getting students to interpret an image partially covered with squares; then taking the squares away and inviting fresh interpretations

- grids – placing a grid on a clear acetate sheet over an image and asking students to 'read' the image square by square; this can support the analysis of part–whole relationships.

> *I had not thought about cognitive conflict in my lessons until I attended the Learning and Teaching Group. It has completely changed the way in which I plan and teach my lessons, ensuring that students are challenged to develop their thinking skills. The response from the students has been fantastic!'*

Linda Griffin, Head of Mathematics, saltash.net community school

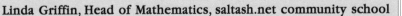

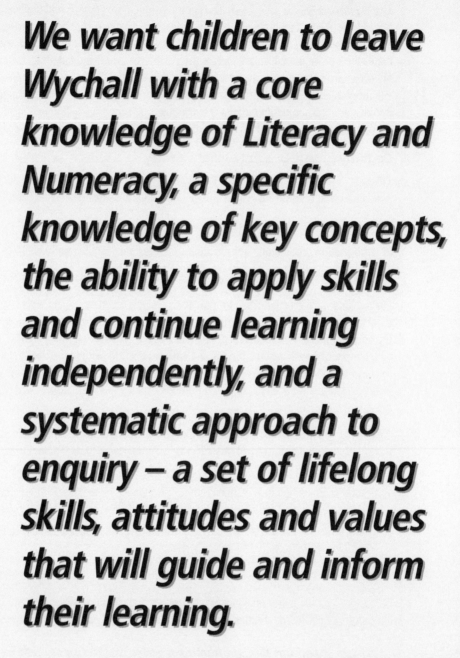

We want children to leave Wychall with a core knowledge of Literacy and Numeracy, a specific knowledge of key concepts, the ability to apply skills and continue learning independently, and a systematic approach to enquiry – a set of lifelong skills, attitudes and values that will guide and inform their learning.

Wychall Primary School

Example: Wychall Primary School, Birmingham – *focus on learner-led learning*

All the staff at the school contributed to this section.

Background

- 3–11 Primary school
- NOR 280
- serving an area that, in terms of deprivation, is in bottom 10% in the country

Catalyst for change

Although we were a successful school, we became increasingly aware that:

- students were successful in tests and could clearly remember the things they had learned, but had real difficulty when the information was presented differently or used in another context – in short, students were retaining knowledge but we were not teaching them to think

- both curriculum and assessment structures resulted in students remembering facts but not learning or practising skills that encouraged them to explore, ask questions, find things out, solve problems or share and explain their ideas

- both staff and Governors felt that the current QCA curriculum with discreet subjects did not allow students to develop enquiry skills and encourage independent learning – students were not being given sufficient opportunity to make links and connections between key concepts.

Step 1 – key skills

As a starting point, we identified key skills for each subject and grouped these by year group.

Cross-phase groups met to identify common themes and ensure continuity and progression.

This allowed us to develop thematic topics, through which to deliver the new curriculum. However, although this enabled students to explore and see the connections between concepts, the question remained, *Is this sufficient to ensure that students develop into effective inquirers, critical thinkers and independent learners?*

We want children to leave Wychall with a core knowledge of Literacy and Numeracy, a specific knowledge of key concepts, the ability to apply skills and continue learning independently, and a systematic approach to enquiry – a set of lifelong skills, attitudes and values that will guide and inform their learning.

It seemed that in order to achieve this we would have to change not only our curriculum, but also our teaching approach.

The 5 'E's:

1 Engage

2 Explore

3 Evaluate

4 Elaborate

5 Explain

Wychall Primary School

Step 2 – 5 'E's

We began by examining a number of curriculum frameworks from other countries, including New Basics, Government of Hong Kong and Missouri Framework for Science. All offered something and we identified teaching processes that we used in part, but we concluded that alone they were insufficient to meet our aspirations for teaching and learning across the curriculum. The result was that we developed and then implemented an approach to thinking known as the *5 'E's*.

The 5 'E's are:

1 Engage

2 Explore

3 Evaluate

4 Elaborate

5 Explain

At the heart of the 5 'E's framework lies the desire to move from the *teacher* driving learning to the *learner* driving learning. Learning is broadly based around a theme, such as Kings and Queens, Pirates of the Caribbean, Great Inventors, and so on, with each theme including aspects of many discrete curriculum areas. Flexibility is important and teachers are encouraged to both respond to what the learner brings and think creatively.

In a nutshell, we find out what the students already know about a particular topic, discover what they would *like* to know, and plan our curriculum accordingly. In this way, teaching is a response to learning and the learner, rather than the other way around.

1 Engage

The first step is the vehicle that drives the topic, as it provides students with a chance to discover what they are interested in, and allows the teacher to assess where the students currently are in terms of knowledge and understanding. At this stage, students should be considering five main questions:

- *What do I already know?*

- *What do I want to find out?*

- *How will I find out? What tools might I use?*

- *What do I think will happen?* (Predict)

- *Why do I want to find out? What am I going to gain?*

The initial stimulus is up to the individual teacher. For example, to launch our space topic, we created a scene to give the impression that an unknown species had crash-landed in our classroom. Clues and evidence were left for students to develop questions, reason, interpret and interrogate, which would then allow us to drive forward a line of enquiry.

The Coloured Paper Process

The Coloured Paper Process is the way in which we launch a topic and construct a framework for learning. The children's ideas, thoughts and questions at each stage of the process are recorded on paper of both a different colour and a different size. All the paper is then assembled in a concentric pattern. The result looks something like an archery target constructed from oblongs rather than circles!

1 The initial stimulus for our learning may come from a visit, picture, artefact, visitor, and so on. If, for example, the stimulus is a picture, it would be displayed in the centre of a sheet of coloured paper.

2 The first sheet is placed upon a larger sheet of paper of a different colour. We pose the question, *What do we already know about this?* and record the responses around the edge of the paper.

3 The 'map' so far is then placed on an even larger sheet of paper, again of a different colour. We then pose the question, *What do we want to know?* and record the responses around the edge of the paper.

4 The process is repeated again by placing the whole thing on an even larger sheet of paper. We now consider *How can we find out the answers to the questions posed in step 3?* Our thoughts are once again recorded on the edge of the paper.

We end up with a large visual display of what we know, what we would like to find out and how we are going to do it.

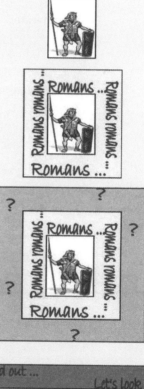

Wychall Primary School

2 Explore

This step, which usually – but not always – follows the 'engage' step, is based upon students finding out, experimenting and deducing information through a wide range of activities. The variety of activities is crucial as we aim to appeal to a range of different learning styles. Individual teachers are responsible for devising interesting and engaging activities, although a bank of activities is being collated for future use.

As this step is central to our new curriculum, it often takes up the lion's share of the time and needs careful planning and consideration. Allowing students to explore in an independent yet structured way also demands that we teach students to explore effectively by introducing them to a wide range of investigative and research tools. However, in many respects this step is just the beginning and provides the platform for students to ask further questions to build on what they have discovered. We are constantly emphasising that the fact that students know something doesn't necessarily mean that they understand it.

3 Evaluate

This step should be carried out after every stage of the framework, to encourage students to reflect upon and justify what they have found out, why they have come to that conclusion, and so on. 'Evaluate' goes hand in hand with 'exploring', as any information or conclusion must be checked out to see if it is correct and reliable.

Sometimes, encouraging students to constantly evaluate their ideas or thoughts can be tricky as some students have little confidence in sharing and articulating their initial ideas when they still lack conclusive evidence to back them up. Interestingly, the same students are constantly trying to justify their words and actions when they think they may be in trouble and this step is exactly the same – getting students to justify and compare.

It can therefore be helpful to have a bank of evaluative statements on display to act as prompts – for example, *What if? Has it worked? Why not? How can I improve it? Was that the best tool? Is there an alternative?*

For the 5 'E's framework to work effectively, students need to be constantly questioning reliability, justifying their thinking, making comparisons and being prepared to try another way if they don't succeed.

4 Elaborate

This step allows students to build upon the basic information and facts that they have discovered. It is an opportunity to really question, deduce and make connections. It is important that we develop this analytical thinking so that students will become increasingly effective at expanding their knowledge and deepening their understanding of the information they have discovered or been taught. In some respects, this is the step that enables students to really develop understanding and consolidate their learning.

As part of this step, students may question their approach and the tool they have been using in the 'explore' step. They may also have discovered the answer to a scientific question during their investigation and now extend their conclusion into a further investigation. When this happens, students begin the 5 'E's process again.

This step should be completed by all students, although the higher order thinking skills involved provide an obvious opportunity for more able students to pursue any alternative lines of enquiry that arose during the initial 'engage' step.

We find out what the students already know about a particular topic, discover what they would like to know, and plan our curriculum accordingly. In this way, teaching is a response to learning and the learner, rather than the other way around.

Wychall Primary School

5 Explain

This step gives students the opportunity to communicate their findings. This should be done in a variety of ways – written, oral, through drama, using ICT, and so on.

This is the opportunity for students and their teacher to assess and evaluate their understanding of a concept and address whether they have achieved a particular key skill linked to the topic. It is also an ideal opportunity to develop speaking, listening and writing skills.

The key to success in this step is variety. A wide range of tools and methods can be used to demonstrate, record and assess what students have investigated and discovered. This step can be completed individually, in small groups (which also promotes teamwork) or in larger groups (which gets students used to working with a range of people and abilities).

Students are given guidance about the various approaches and tools available to them in this step, and gradually encouraged to select the most appropriate way of communicating their research.

Outcomes

Since the introduction of the 5 'E's framework, teachers report that:

- students are finding the approach far more challenging
- students are increasingly able to make connections for themselves
- motivation levels are significantly higher.

The students report that:

- *It gets harder as you are going along, but you don't notice it because it's fun.*
- *I can research in more detail.*
- *We spend less time on the carpet and more time learning things.*

Reflect

Which best describes your classroom:

- teacher driven?
- learner led?

Those who try to build the present in the image of the past will miss out entirely on the challenge of the future.

Winston Churchill

The end of the beginning

There is a real feeling in education these days that we have come to the end of the beginning. For we have just lived through a concerted national effort to improve *teaching* and raise standards. The strategy – largely based upon training, monitoring, feedback and intervention, and conducted against a backdrop of intense pressure and public accountability – has for the most part been successful; the quality of teaching has significantly improved and examination results have risen in a great many schools.

The challenge is now twofold: firstly, to sustain these improvements and continue to move forward from a now high baseline, and secondly to switch the focus firmly on to *learning*. The key question, and the one that this book has sought to address is, **Will the strategies and policies that have enabled us to get to good and improve *teaching* be sufficient to help us move beyond good and promote *learning*?**

The easy answer, certainly in the short term, is quite probably *yes*. Many schools have found the recipe for examination and inspection success, and there is an understandable temptation to adopt the 'if it ain't broke' mentality. However, for how much longer will the 'training, monitoring, telling' approach enable schools to *sustain improvement*? This is an important phrase; sustaining improvement is not the same as maintaining high standards. Is it to be more of the same, or do we need a change of emphasis if we are to break through the inevitable plateau of attainment and achievement?

Michael Fullan contends that improvement is cyclical – there is an initial improvement followed by a plateau or levelling off. He argues that the plateau effect is not simply the result of burn-out; rather, he suggests that *the strategies that brought initial success are not the ones – not powerful enough – to take us to higher levels.*

This book has suggested that we have reached the end of the beginning and that the time has come to take the next step. It has argued that **the future, in terms of both pedagogy and policy, demands an approach rooted in learning**.

More specifically, it has suggested that:

- everything that we do must be based explicitly upon learning

- teachers must be learners too

- we have a professional responsibility to go on learning about learning. We must reflect on it, discuss it and unpack it, in order to deepen our understanding of it; because the better we understand learning and the learning process, the better able we are to facilitate it in others.

- The more we know about learning, the better able we are to facilitate it in others.

- You can be taught to teach, but you have to learn about learning.

- This means that teachers need to be learners too.

- If we want teachers to be learners we first have to create a climate conducive to learning.

- Emotion is the barrier to reflection. Judgements provoke an emotional response.

- We seek a culture based on professional dialogue and personal reflection. Such a culture can be sparked and driven by non-judgemental data.

- If we want to look for different things, we have to look through different eyes.

- Teacher Enquiry / Action Research and Coaching have key roles to play. Both are rooted in learning.

- Much 'coaching' that is currently taking place in schools is at best extremely limited, and at worst isn't coaching at all.

  - Coaching is a non-judgemental process – this is the core, distinctive principle – yet much 'coaching' in schools is predicated on judgements. Often it is something the best teachers do to the weaker ones.

  - There is a pressing need to invest in on-going programmes to coach the coaches. A day's training will not lead to high-quality coaching taking place.

  - Coaching is a philosophy, not an event. Coaching has the potential to influence, and even become the culture. And if coaching is rooted in learning ...

It may seem a little like stating the obvious. However:

1   Learning will not just assume centre-stage. It will become the focus only if we make it so. In other words, if we want learning in the spotlight, we have to place it there. This involves firstly making a conscious commitment to making it the main thing in both the classroom and at whole-school level, and secondly maintaining that commitment in the face of all distractions.

2   We must be aware what a significant shift in emphasis this is. For we have lived through a decade in which success, for both schools and students, has not been dependent upon learning – certainly not at any deep, meaningful level. Teachers have simply been required to teach while students have been required to pass exams. A genuine focus upon learning will have far-reaching implications for both pedagogy in the classroom and policy and procedures at whole-school level and beyond.

Much of the national drive to raise standards has focused upon teaching. This is not a criticism; there is an argument that this was the necessary first step. The questions we must now address are, *Is it now time to take the second step?* and, if so, *In which direction should that step be?*

This book has argued that the time has indeed come to take the important second step and that our compass must be reset towards learning. These words are neither new nor radical – indeed they are nothing less than national policy – yet in order to mean anything, we must move beyond rhetoric. Everybody may be talking about learning, learning schools and reflective practitioners, yet whether or not we are successful in placing learning centre-stage will depend upon the extent to which we can translate these fine words into action.

The way forward

A future based on learning demands that we first know what it looks like. Our collective attention must therefore swing away from syllabus and structures and focus firmly upon substance. We have talked about lessons for long enough; now is the time to talk about learning. We have done the Inset day on starters and followed it up with another on plenaries; they were necessary and useful but now is the time to move on and unpack the middle. Now is the time to learn more about learning. And here lies the crux; for **while you can teach people to teach, you have to learn about learning**.

In many respects, switching the emphasis in classrooms, from children being taught to children both learning and learning about learning, begins with teachers being learners and learning more about learning. It is a symbiotic relationship.

- Teaching quality has improved significantly in recent years; the challenge now is to move 'beyond good'.

- In particular, tasks and activities have improved and children are generally more active in lessons. The next steps are:
    - ensuring that increased activity is matched by increased reflection; reflecting on what was learned, and how it was learned, is the key to better learning and better learners
    - a focus on interaction; the task may be the catalyst but the real learning takes place when children interact with the task and each other
    - the learning process is mediated by the teacher; great teachers know when and how to intervene.

- To improve learning still further we must therefore focus on:
    - reflection
    - interaction
    - intervention

- Good teachers engage students; great teachers:
    - Entice
    - Excite
    - Enthral

- To entice, excite and enthral we must focus on the C words:
    - Confusion
    - Curiosity
    - Challenge
    - Creativity

Yet this may be easier said than done; for learning rarely flowers in stony soil. If the seeds of dialogue, reflection, collaboration and the *desire* to go on *improving* are to take root, flourish and eventually bloom, the soil must be fertile and rich in respect and trust. They will not prosper in impoverished conditions, strangled by the thistles that are suspicion, justification and the *necessity* to continually *prove* competence. An atmosphere that contains a healthy balance of challenge and support is very different from one that is saturated in pressure and accountability.

Yet many teachers are operating in an atmosphere of intense pressure, spend Inset days doing little more than listen to a trainer, and participate in a monitoring procedure that is limited to them being observed and receiving feedback. It may have been an effective blueprint to standardise and improve teaching and to raise the examination result bar but hardly the recipe for sustained and significant learning.

To be fair, it is an approach that was not designed to lead to learning; the role of the teacher during phase one of the improvement drive has largely been limited to being taught and teaching. This approach served a purpose but will be insufficient if we are serious about placing learning centre-stage, turning good lessons into great ones and sustaining and building upon the gains of the recent past. Learning is the way forward and it therefore follows that our first priority must be to create a climate conducive to learning – for teachers as well as children.

If this is accepted, then Senior School Leaders have a clear route forward; their first, and major task, must be to create the climate. Never mind that weather conditions nationally are largely unfavourable, those in senior positions must exert their influence to create the micro-climate in which teachers can be learners. The key word here is *create*; for climates are created, consciously or otherwise, and are the result of a million words, actions, policies and procedures that simultaneously reflect the climate and contribute to it. It may be a daunting prospect – many in the profession feel battered and bruised – and Headteachers may be forgiven for thinking that they are swimming against the tide, but it is a challenge that must be met if we are serious about learning being the main thing for teachers as well as children.

Learning, deep learning, is heavily dependent upon personal reflection. Emotion is the fog that can so easily prevent people from seeing things as they are – as such, it is a barrier to reflection. If we aspire to a school of reflective practitioners that talk, swap, share, disagree, take risks and generally push back the boundaries, then we first have to lift the emotional fog. In practical terms, this means removing, or at least reducing, the unremitting focus on judgements and replace it with non-judgemental data. For non-judgemental data, rather than provoking an emotional, defensive reaction, can both spark and fan the flames of reflection and dialogue and ultimately lead to meaningful and sustained

Traditional teaching was about giving students the picture; facilitating learning is about helping them join the dots.

This does not mean that teachers are never judged. There is no call for a return to the days where teachers operated in splendid isolation. It has not been suggested that we abandon the strategies that have enabled the profession to take significant steps forward; rather, that if we wish to maintain the momentum we need a change of emphasis. This does not mean that teachers are never monitored, never receive feedback and never attend training; simply that the emphasis must switch from monitoring, feedback and training to reflection, dialogue and coaching.

The changing paradigm

The times, as Bob Dylan told us, are changing. By putting learning centre-stage, we are in the process of redefining what we mean by excellent teaching. As Paul Ginnis puts it in the foreword (page 5), the paradigm is beginning to shift. In simple terms, lessons that would once have been considered perfectly acceptable would no longer pass muster for failing the sixty-four-thousand-dollar question, *What have they learned?* The role that was once limited to telling, showing and checking has evolved into *facilitating learning*. If the past was box A on the TIMS grid (see page 112) the future is most definitely box D.

If the paradigm is shifting, so too the context; the challenge to deal with unsatisfactory teaching has been met, there is a consistency in classrooms and what might be termed the 'nuts and bolts' of the job are generally done well. Putting teaching under the microscope for a moment, we would see that the specific nuts and bolts that have been tightened and polished are the way in which lessons are structured and the quality of the tasks employed. At the risk of being repetitive, it should be emphasised that this is not a criticism – there was a time, and not that long ago, when children spent long hours copying from the blackboard. However, sorting out teaching was not the ultimate destination, just the necessary first step, and we return again to the central question of this book, *Is it now time to move on?*

Our end goal was not to improve teaching but to enhance learning, and this is where our attention must now turn. Two aspects in particular of what may loosely be termed facilitating learning demand our collective and focused attention:

● interaction

● intervention.

For if the environment, structure and task provide the context and catalyst, the real learning is dependent on the way learners interact and reflect, and the way in which the process is mediated by the teacher. The fact that these dimensions have a nebulous quality and are undeniably difficult to pin down and measure must not deter us, for these are the elements that hold the key to deep, meaningful learning.

As soon as we accept a sound approach to learning, one based on constructivism, the psychology of motivation and the central place of emotion, there have to be concomitant changes to the way business is conducted in the classroom – **the teaching paradigm must alter.**

Paul Ginnis

Such learning is exciting, messy, often spontaneous and deeply personal. Yet many lessons these days, while hugely competent, have become predictable, formulaic and safe. Maybe, as Paul Ginnis suggests, this was the price that we had to pay for standardising teaching. Our challenge is how to make learning unpredictable, captivating and above all *fun* – without losing the undoubted gains of recent years.

Much is known about teaching (box A of the TIMS grid). We do that well. Far less is known about mediating the learning of others (box D), yet this is the future and this is where our attention must turn. Our professional vocabulary has expanded considerably in recent years. Talk of facilitating learning, scaffolding and mediation are common-place. Yet, as any school pupil studying French will testify, the ability to recite the words and regurgitate the phrases does not mean that you understand the language.

The challenge is to get beneath the skin of the new rhetoric; to learn about learning and understand understanding. More importantly, to understand it sufficiently well so that we can facilitate it in others. It is the next stage of the on-going narrative. The drive to improve teaching was just the first chapter. It was largely written for us; all that was required of teachers was to read it and respond. This passage is now drawing to a conclusion and we are about to embark on chapter two, which will focus firmly on learning. It is a pivotal moment, not least because it is a chapter that the profession can write – or at least contribute to– for itself.

It an enticing prospect. But it will be far from easy, not least because learning is, as John Abbott puts it, *the most gloriously messy, unstructured, mysterious process known to man.*

It is for this reason, because learning has an intangible, abstract and elusive quality, that learning about learning requires a structure and a focus. We need to find a way of breaking through the complexity.

The TIMS grid (page 112) is a corner stone of this book and is designed to do just that. It is a simplified model of a highly complex reality, and was designed to help people deepen their understanding of the learning process. It is a grid you must unpack for yourself. *You* have to explore it, talk about it, grapple with it and reflect upon it because learning involves making personal sense. Meaning cannot be given to you.

Young people deserve teachers who have the confidence to learn and to improve, just as teachers deserve schools which help them learn and improve.

Scottish Consultative Council on the Curriculum

While plotting a course to steer us through the next set of challenges, this book has also acknowledged that schools are still operating in the dichotomy that is education. We talk of learning yet we measure schools, students and teachers by examination success, we talk of developing the capacity of individuals yet we know that spoon-feeding will get sufficient numbers through sufficient hoops, we strive to invest in strategies that will yield long-term sustainable improvement yet are pressurised for immediate and measurable success and we talk of the need for teachers to be learners yet create an environment that couldn't be less conducive to learning if we tried.

Which brings us full circle; learning will not just assume centre-stage. It will become the focus only if we make it so. In other words, if we want learning in the spotlight, we have to place it there and this involves firstly making a conscious commitment to making it the main thing in both the classroom and at whole school-level, and secondly maintaining that commitment in the face of all distractions.

Stephen Covey argues that success is dependent upon keeping the main thing the main thing. And for us, **the main thing is, and always will be ... learning**.

> **Reflect**
>
> ● What have been the most significant points raised by this book?
>
> ● What do you do differently as a result of reading it?
>
> ● What do you do first?

Further reading

Below are listed titles referred to in *And the Main Thing is ... Learning*, as well as other useful publications.

Coaching

Coaching for Performance John Whitmore (Nicholas Brealey Publishing, 1992; third edition, 2003)

Effective Coaching Myles Downey (Texere, London, 1999)

Coaching – Evoking Excellence in Others James Flaherty (Butterworth-Heinemann, Burlington USA, 1999)

Co-Active Coaching Laura Whitworth, Henry Kimsey-House, Phil Sandahl Davies (Black Publishing, California, 1998)

Leadership

Leadership and Professional Development in Schools John West-Burnham and Fergus O'Sullivan (Pearson Education Limited, 1998)

The New Leaders Daniel Goleman (Little Brown, 2002)

Smart Schools David Perkins (The Free Press, 1992)

Change Forces Michael Fullan (Falmer Press, 1993)

The Challenge of School Change Michael Fullan (Skylight Professional Development, 1997)

Schools that Learn Peter Senge et al (Nicholas Brealey Publishing, 2000)

The Intelligent School Barbara MacGilchrist, Kate Myers, Jane Reed (Sage Publications, 2004)

The Inner Game of Tennis W. Timothy Gallwey (Pan, 1986)

First Things First Stephen R. Covey, A Roger Merrill and Rebecca R Merrill (Simon and Schuster, 1994)

Seven Habits of Highly Effective People Stephen R. Covey (Simon and Schuster, 1989)

The Self Evaluation File John MacBeath (Learning Files, Scotland)

Schools Must Speak for Themselves John MacBeath (Routledge, 1999)

Organization Development Richard Beckhard (Addison-Wesley, 1969)

Learning

Building Learning Power Guy Claxton (TLO, 2002)

Teaching Children to Think Robert Fisher (Basil Blackwell, 1990)

The Unfinished Revolution John Abbott and Terry Ryan (Network Educational Press, 2000)

Self-Theories: their role in motivation, personality and development Carol S. Dweck (Psychology Press, 2000)

How Children Fail John Holt (Pelican Books, 1969)

Superteaching Eric Jensen (Turning Point Publishing USA, 1994)

The Teacher's Toolkit Paul Ginnis (Crown House Publishing, 2002)

Thought and Language Lev Vygotsky (MIT Press, 1973)

Effective Learning Chris Watkins et al (*Institute of Education Research Matters*, summer 2002)

Learning about Learning Enhances Performance Chris Watkins et al (*Institute of Education Research Matters*, spring 2001)

Effective Learning in Schools Christopher Bowring-Carr and John West-Burnham (Pearson Education, 1997)

Learning Intelligence edited by Michael Shayer and Philip Adey (Open University Press, 2002)

Really Raising Standards Philip Adey and Michael Shayer (Routledge, 1994)

Teaching for Effective Learning (Scottish CCC, 1996)

Pedagogy and Practice: Teaching and Learning in Secondary Schools (DfES, 2004)

Beyond Teaching and Learning Win Wenger (Project Renaissance, 1992)

Effective Teaching: Evidence and Practice Daniel Muijs and David Reynolds (Paul Chapman Publications, 2001)

Other books by Mike Hughes

Tweak to Transform – Improving teaching: A practical handbook for school leaders (Network Continuum, 2002)

Strategies for Closing the Learning Gap (Network Continuum, 2001)

Closing the Learning Gap (Network Continuum, 1999)

Lessons are for Learning (Network Continuum, first published 1997, reprinted and updated 2005)

These books, and a comprehensive range of other titles and educational resources, are available from Network Continuum:

T: 01202 665432

W: www.networkcontinuum.co.uk

Learning Files, Scotland

For further information about *The Self-Evaluation File* by Professor John MacBeath:

T: 0141 6395836

W: www.learningfilescotland.co.uk

CASE, CAME, CATE

For further information about *Cognitive Acceleration through Science Education, Cognitive Acceleration through Maths Education* and *Cognitive Acceleration through Technology Education* programmes referred to in Section 5, including suggested resources, Professional Development opportunities and further links:

W: www.kcl.ac.uk/schools/sspp/education/research/cognitive.html

Thinking Through

For further information about the *Thinking Through* books referred to in Section 5:

T: Chris Kington Publishing, 020 7954 3474

W: www.chriskingtonpublishing.co.uk

Mike Hughes Education Training and Support

Coaching the Coaches

There is currently considerable interest in the role of coaching in schools. This is not surprising as the evidence continues to grow that coaching is by far the most effective way of helping teachers improve and develop their practice!

However ...

1   Coaching in schools is sometimes limited in scope. Often it involves a lesson observation and a feedback session and can easily be perceived as a support mechanism for weaker teachers. While this approach has a place, it is important to acknowledge that coaching is much more than this. **Coaching is an approach that can permeate the entire institution and release the latent potential of all (teachers *and* children).**

2   It is not coaching that improves the quality of teaching and ultimately learning, it is *high-quality* coaching, and there is the key question to consider of **Who coaches the coaches?**

We offer:

- a three-day sandwich *Coaching the Coaches* Programme (two consecutive days followed by a third day one term later)
- coaching master classes
- *Coaching the Trainer* – developing training skills for those charged with training coaches
- developing students as coaches (from key stage one upwards)
- the opportunity to gain accreditation at master's level
- customised programmes to fit in with your on-going CPD programme

Key components:

- The **why** and the **what** of coaching
- Coaching and reflective practitioners
- Observation for coaching
- From feedback to professional dialogue
- Structuring the coaching session
- Developing key coaching skills
- Listening to understand
- Working with reluctant colleagues
- Getting started

For more information about coaching services, contact:
Education Training and Support, PO Box 797, Cheltenham, GL52 6WR
T: 01242 238990   E: msh.hughes@virgin.net   W: www.mikehughes-ets.co.uk

Another Smile For Monday Morning

Wouldn't it be great if people came to work on a Monday laughing and smiling? What a terrific way to start the week. What a happy place the staff room would be!

Another Smile for Monday Morning is the sequel to *A Smile for Monday Morning* and is designed to help teachers start the week on a cheerful note. It contains 40 cartoons, all with an educational flavour, which can be used on your staff notice board or weekly bulletin. Look at Ofsted, the DfES and National Strategies in a new light and begin the week by sharing a smile and a joke with your colleagues.

Another Smile for Monday Morning is priced £9.99 (+ £2 p&p). To obtain a copy send a cheque payable to **RH Products** to RH Products, PO Box 797, Cheltenham GL52 6WR.